Spooky Creepy Baltimore County

D. P. Roseberry

Schiffer Publishing Ltd
4880 Lower Valley Road, Atglen, Pennsylvania 19310

† The contemporary stories that follow are based on true hauntings, though the people involved have chosen to remain anonymous; and for that reason, I've changed names to protect the innocent—or not so innocent. Though the facts are accurate to the best of my knowledge, it's important to note that I have also dramatized the stories a bit for the sake of dialog and campfire reading. I hope you enjoy these haunting tales and tell them during your own campfire sessions!

Schiffer Books are available at special discounts for bulk purchases for sales promotions or premiums. Special editions, including personalized covers, corporate imprints, and excerpts can be created in large quantities for special needs. For more information contact the publisher:

Published by Schiffer Publishing Ltd.
4880 Lower Valley Road
Atglen, PA 19310
Phone: (610) 593-1777; Fax: (610) 593-2002
E-mail: Info@schifferbooks.com

For the largest selection of fine reference books on this and
related subjects, please visit our web site at
www.schifferbooks.com
We are always looking for people to write books on new and related subjects.
If you have an idea for a book please contact us at the above address.

This book may be purchased from the publisher.
Include $5.00 for shipping.
Please try your bookstore first.
You may write for a free catalog.

In Europe, Schiffer books are distributed by
Bushwood Books
6 Marksbury Ave.
Kew Gardens
Surrey TW9 4JF England
Phone: 44 (0) 20 8392-8585; Fax: 44 (0) 20 8392-9876
E-mail: info@bushwoodbooks.co.uk
Website: www.bushwoodbooks.co.uk
Free postage in the U.K., Europe; air mail at cost.

Other Schiffer Books by D. P. Roseberry
Cape May Haunts, 978-0-7643-2821-3, $14.95
Spooky York, Pennsylvania, 978-0-7643-3021-6, $14.99
Ghosts of Valley Forge and Phoenixville, 978-0-7643-2633-2, $14.95

Other Schiffer Books on Related Subjects
Baltimore Harbor Haunts, 0-7643-2304-0, $14.95

Library of Congress Control Number: 2008943104

Designed by Mark David Bowyer
Type set in Grasshopper / New Baskerville BT

ISBN: 978-0-7643-3254-8
Printed in the United States of America

Contents

Dedication

For Grandmother Gill, alive and kicking criminals to the curb in the next world. George and JC who died too young. For Aunt Dorothy, Uncle Lewis, Aunt Jessie, Steve, my other three grandparents, and every animal in the pet cemetery dug at the rear of my parents' house—and, of course, my Tessa—you are missed. For *all* my spirits—you know who you are—this is for you!

Acknowledgments

My mother and father were the beginning source of my interest in the paranormal and my encouragement through the years. Also, my husband, who I continually drag around to take photos (and who quietly puts up with ghostly shenanigans at home). My daughter and granddaughter who don't think I'm all that nuts to believe in these things. Darlene, the best friend one could hope for and a true confidant in the quest for the paranormal. To Laurie Hull, ever a partner in ghostly research. And all the folks in the stories that follow. Thank you.

Introduction

Ghostly Phenomena

"Be careful when navigating this terrain, for this might be the place of the paranormal experience."

— Isaac Davis, III, Investigator for
Chester County Paranormal Research Society

** Most of the following story was from my first ghost book (Ghosts of Valley Forge and Phoenixville) as an introduction to how I became involved in ghosts. But since the whole thing occurred when I was a younger soul living and growing up in Baltimore County, I thought it would be appropriate to tell it here!*

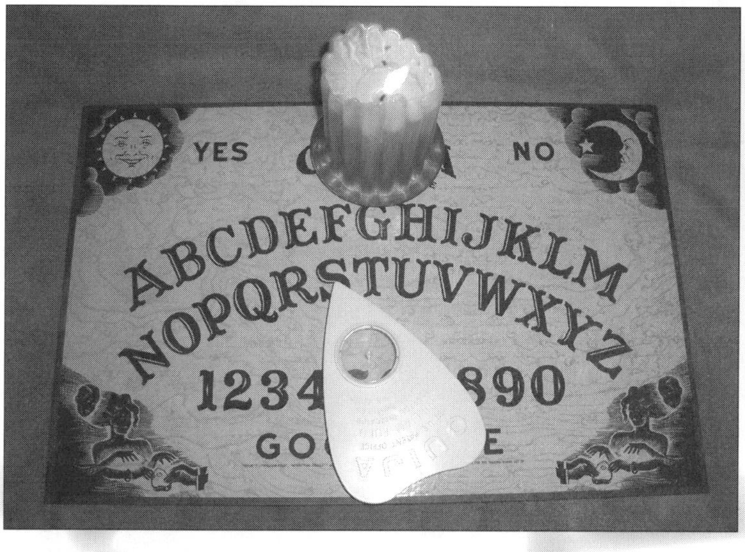

With this ghost book — my fourth one— I have to laugh, because I've finally learned that even understanding the world of paranormal—and ghosts in particular—takes a lot of stair-step learning that begins much further back than one might initially remember. So many things in our lives these days and in times of old are pushed to the recesses of the mind, put on the back-burner, shoved into the proverbial dark closet not to be opened until there was time to think. If there ever *was*, indeed, time to think.

In my first book, *Ghosts of Valley Forge and Phoenixville*, I went back a little bit into my own life and thought about some of the occurrences that made me believe in ghosts early on. But I didn't examine them in any real depth. I think I was still stuck in that mode of "13 Ghosts" (the black and white cinema version) and "House on Haunted Hill" (the old movie, of course). The fact was, though, I'd had lots of paranormal experiences and was told many stories of real hauntings—they were just on back burner, till now.

I first touched the ghostly world at the tender age of fifteen while at a pajama party attended by several of my closest crazy friends held at a house in the neighborhood right behind (what was called then) the Garrison Police Station—now Precinct 13. Alas, most girls at fifteen participating in this kind of social gathering can be called crazy to some degree. The parties and the questionable behavior that takes place at these events is a ritual—a rite of passage, a girl gathering of gibberish and playful antics that seem so important at the time. Though I know that most people have a clear understanding of the nature of such a party, let me say that we were a gaggle of girls, intent on raising hell for the better part of a night into the wee morning hours—a nightmare to sane chaperoning adults. This, then, was the setting for my very first ghostly "encounter."

Naturally high on caffeine-filled soda and salty potato chips, our hostess pulled out a marvel-of-the-time toy Ouija (wee-gee)

Board that was hidden deep in the back of her closet behind the winter coats and stacks of *Life* magazine. Back then, none of us had a notion that this paranormal contraption, used to tell the future, might be dangerous or, at the very least, unsettling as is taught today by some psychics and those with intuitive ability. Rather, it was a way to find out who we would marry, when our first *real* loves would arrive, and whether the latest teen heart-throb would find his way to Owings Mills, Maryland (and vicinity), to sweep one of us up onto a white charger and ride into the clouds for that life of happily-ever-after. (Ah, youth.)

At first, the entertainment aspect of this "toy" was questionable. The planchette (a triangular little device held up by two casters and a vertical pointer that, when lightly touched by two sets of fingertips, spelled out messages that could be seen letter by letter through a clear round opening on the top of the triangle) would not move. One by one, we switched places around the board until it found the two people who seemed most suitable for a supernatural encounter. Of course, yours truly and my close friend (whose identity I shall protect, least she be reminded of this strange night and object to having her good name plastered about the world for merely being part of this supernatural experience) were the chosen ones.

As our fingers rested on the planchette, it started to spell words by moving around the lettered board—slowly at first, and then much more quickly. The spirit in the board found us appealing enough to talk in general girly gibberish for a while. It was fun.

The other girls accused us right away of deception. They believed that we were moving the planchette ourselves—pushing it with our fingertips to spell the words we wanted to see. This was a hoax, a cheap trick to make them think that the answers given by the board were real! After all, some of the predictions were less than attractive to the young ears of those listening. (No one liked the idea of growing up and having children at this stage in life. Who needed to know *that* kind of thing at fifteen?)

My friend and I were both angered by our other friends' attacks, and we responded by truthfully whining, "We're not moving it! This is real!" And it was true; we weren't moving it. It *was* real. The board had a mind of its own. (Hmmm. A board with a mind. Sounds suspicious to me even at this late date. And a bit scary, too.)

But all was not to proceed in such a fun-loving fashion for very long. It was about this time that the board became...belligerent. Though I don't recall the predications, discussion, or too many of the bad words that followed to make us feel the malevolent aura that the activity had taken on, I do remember the climatic incident that convinced me that there was, indeed, a ghostly dimension beyond the one I knew.

Our stereo was booming quite loudly during this activity—the latest Beatles album. (Yes, this was before CDs were thought of, and we were using record players to play vinyl albums.) The group's steady beat offered a symbolic background to our laughing teenage group. It was an easy time—a time of little care and a time of boys with Beatles haircuts.

My fingers continued to rest lightly on the planchette as did those of my friend. We'd asked a question. It wasn't an important question, as I recall. Trivial. Probably even silly. But no answer materialized on the board in front of us. The planchette sat still. We asked another question. Still nothing. The crowd around us was becoming restless and bored. (Attention spans were not lengthy at this age.)

But then the planchette began moving in small loops. Tight little circles. I could feel a rush of...*something*...go through my fingers. I question it even as I write about it now. Was this feeling really there? Had I imagined it?

An electric anger seemed to pulse from the planchette as it began to speed up, moving round and round in larger and larger circles. That tingly sensation moved up my fingers to my hands and arms. Gooseflesh erupted. When I looked up from the board to my friend's eyes, I found her looking at me in the same fearful wonder that I was feeling. This was bizarre.

The planchette finally began to spell. Each letter was chosen with quick jerks; and the girls around us spelled out loud as it sped across the board.

T U R N O F F T H E M U S I C

The planchette spelled; and then respelled and respelled and respelled. Faster and faster. *Turn off the music.*

One of the girls called out with a laugh, "If you don't like the music, turn it off yourself!"

When she spoke the challenge, my friend and I pulled our hands away from the planchette as though we'd been burned. This was not good. We both felt it and just sat there in silence. Waiting. No one there believed that we were really getting messages from beyond—from some *place* and some*one* not living. Not breathing. Not part of the festivities.

But *we* knew that we were not moving the device ourselves. We were the *only* ones who positively knew this. Our eyes were big with distress, and gooseflesh remained on our arms. We knew instinctively that something was about to happen that would change our beliefs about ghosts and the world beyond life.

Suddenly the lights in the room dimmed and then brightened again. The Beatles album began to drag on the phonograph as the turntable slowed, their voices pulled out in low groaning growls of sound. Then the phonograph completely stopped, the tone arm remaining stately in the middle of the record as if it were waiting to start up again once someone brought the power back.

But the power was there. Lights blazed in the room. Only the phonograph lacked the power to continue. One girl checked the outlet. The record player was plugged in. All was as it should be—except that the music had been turned off.

Silence held the room with a frosty grip. The other girls in our group sat wide-eyed and shocked. (Maybe this wasn't a trick after all!) I got up slowly, took the tone arm off the stopped record, and turned the phonograph switch to *off*. Looking up to the group of girls, I said, "Ditch the Ouija Board." I walked from the room and as far as I know, none of us has spoken of the incident since. At least not me... until this day.

I'm not even sure what happened to the board after that.

It was later that I found that many such incidents had taken place in this particular house in Garrison. These were things that the family living there didn't speak of in public. Too many people disbelieved during that era, fearing that they would be thought strange. This home was a favorite place for hauntings and activity involving mischievous ghosts. I was told that, oftentimes, curtains would open and close without human assistance, strange smells would permeate the halls, babies would laugh at imaginary guests, and sounds of footsteps and chains would awaken the family from a dead sleep at night. It was probably a good thing that I didn't know of such things that first contact night.

At any rate, you can see how my background fits snugly into the ghostly present. So take notes—the following places have varied haunts. And you don't want to miss them.

— D. P. Roseberry

Chapter One

Painters Mill Promises

Painters Mill Apartments, Owings Mills

"Whether people realize it or not, there's a lot more activity going on around us all the time than what the eyes and ears can perceive."
— Marla Brooks, *Ghosts of Hollywood III*

The Power of an Animal

The shop was unassuming, situated at the end of an old strip shopping center in Essex. Though Sandy had been through the area up-teen times during visits to one friend or another, she'd not noticed the little American Indian novelty store. Something drew her to it this sunny Saturday morning. It wasn't as if she had any fascination with Native American décor or any special knowledge of historic heritage; rather it was more of a gentle push from some unseen hands of a source unknown.

Once inside the shop, she hadn't a clue what to look at—nothing particular attracted her—so she just browsed through the pretty jewelry and textiles, wondering why she was there.

Behind the glass counter holding an array of Native treasures, sat an old Indian man on a stool. At first glance, she could see the lines of age on his skin, like cracks bordering a long-dried riverbed that once flourished green with foliage. He watched her every move with interest. She ignored him—it was impolite to stare, even if he was.

Finally, as she meandered back towards the front of the shop where the man sat, he reached down into the display case, pulled out a small box, and placed it on the counter. "This is what you've come for," he said matter-of-factly.

The broken silence surprised Sandy and she walked over to look at the closed box. "What is it?"

The man opened the box and took out the head of a rattlesnake, sitting it gently on the counter. "It has power for you. And a message of caution. It will help you look into the heart of another."

Sandy looked at the snakehead with a grimace on her face. "I don't *think* so," she said, a flip tone to her voice that she hadn't intended. She didn't want to insult the man, but this thing was just wrong. Its gross features and open biting mouth were practically obscene.

The Indian man pushed the head towards her a few inches. "But it has chosen you for a reason," he stated simply. "The snake has a message for your spirit. It tells of transformation and seeks to change the poisons of your body and mind that you will be exposed to in the near future. It will protect you in this time. It speaks to wisdom...and sexual power."

She frowned, but couldn't draw her attention away from the artifact before her, keeping her eyes on it as she spoke back to him. "Are you a psychic? What do you know about my future; and how in the world could a snake be involved? I hate snakes."

"Ah, but the snake does for you what you cannot do for yourself. It sheds its skin and shows you that which lies beneath. It has chosen you."

"So you've said." Sandy still could not take her eyes off the monstrous thing. Its mouth was open and its fangs were poised to bite. She shivered, being able to imagine those fangs sinking into the skin on her forearm. (*I'm definitely watching too much Animal Planet*, she thought to herself.) Surely this was a sales ploy. Yet there was something else. The man's words rang true—*how* she knew that she could not phantom. She'd heard about the wisdom of the Native American people and did not doubt it—they seemed to have a hook to nature that most people had forgotten over the decades of technology and refined thinking. It was a sad loss, to be sure.

"Well, how much is this thing?" she asked, now lowering herself a bit to see it's face more closely.

"This power animal—*your* power animal—is $80."

Oh, this was definitely a sales gimmick. *Good one,* she thought. "Eighty dollars? You've got to be kidding!"

"It is a real animal, not manufactured by the tools of the now. It has a real animal spirit inside it. It has real power for you who needs it. It has chosen you and has called you into my store. Be still and hear its voice."

Looking up into the man's pale eyes, she felt trapped in a trance—but it wasn't a negative thing. It was a connection to the world around her that she'd not before felt. A quiet overtook her busy mind and she strained to hear as he'd suggested. It was then, as though approaching from a distance, that she heard the gentle "*ssssss*" sound of a snake.

Why am I not afraid? she thought, tilting her head in wonder. *I've always been afraid of snakes and reptiles in general…*

The answer to her question was immediately in her head. *I am your power animal for this upcoming battle. Be mindful and listen to my guidance. Keep silent about your knowledge of me. It is to your benefit to be secretive. Tell no one. No one.*

Sandy pulled out her credit card. "Do you take VISA?"

The man smiled. "I do."

Sandy

Sandy peeked through the curtains leading out to her patio door on the third floor of her one-bedroom apartment on the main drag through the Painters Mill Apartments complex. Yup. There was an Indian. Right there at the corner of Dolfield Road and the entrance into the apartments. And he was watching her.

Well, he might not have been watching her exactly. Oh, alright, who was she kidding? This Indian, complete with war paint and a tomahawk was watching her apartment—and more specifically—her. He'd been there since she'd gotten up that morning to take the dog for a walk. Puppers, for some reason, had provided such a demanding...tantrum…to go out before the sun was even up that she'd been coerced into doing the Pupper Run early—pee, poop, quick smell of the playground, done.

Once down the three flights of stairs and onto the common grounds of the complex, both she and Puppers had stopped cold. There he was. Yes, he was really there. Just watching her. He didn't look menacing. Well, other than the fact that it was 5 a.m. and still almost dark and he had war paint on. But she didn't get the feel that he was there to harm her.

Of course, what did she know about anyone wanting to harm anyone? She led a sheltered and happy life without any dismal encounters at all. At twenty-two, she'd finally ventured out on her own (once she'd landed a decent job) and rented this beautiful apartment. True, it was a mere two miles from her parents' home (just in case), and the dishwasher was sporadic in operation, but all in all, her life had been humdrum and moving right along.

The only thing she really missed was adventure—something cool and meaningful to give a punch to the dreary efforts of moving herself from hour to hour, day to day, year to year. This thinking, though present in full vigor when she'd forced herself from her warm bed that fall morning, had dissipated as she strained to see the Indian at the end of the street.

Puppers saw him, too, and had apparently forgotten why they were there and what he was supposed to be doing. And it was odd that the dog didn't bark at the strange figure. Puppers barked at everything and everybody and had almost gotten her kicked out of her apartment for undue noise at odd hours—until she'd put up the baby gate to keep him from being able to slide his little self beyond the curtains at the patio doors, where he was provided with a wonderful view of every car, every person…and every Indian passing by. But as mentioned, he didn't bark at the Indian they saw now. He stared just as Sandy stared.

Without waiting for the dog to do his business, Sandy pulled at the leash and dragged the dog (who was still trying to see the Indian) up the outside stairs of the building and into what she felt was a safe haven. Up the three flights and quickly to her apartment door, she pulled Puppers in after her, slammed the door, and dead bolted it. Puppers would have to pee in the house. Not a pleasant thought, but he'd go on paper if he couldn't get out. She laid down a fresh layer of the newspaper on the linoleum floor in the kitchen. He'd be okay.

Puttering around the apartment, Sandy purposely avoided the draped patio doors and busied herself with packing the dishwasher (hoping it would work), gathering dirty laundry, and considering what she would wear for the date she had that evening. She forced herself to think of other things by cleaning and contemplating the near future—one that didn't hold Indians.

Alas, the patio doors in her living room kept calling to her. *Come, look out. See the Indian on the lawn. He's coming, he's coming.*

So Sandy, puffing herself up in a stance that would tell the world—and hopefully herself—that she was afraid of nothing, deliberately walked to the drapes and pulled them open.

The sun still was not up, but there was light—plenty of light, more than Sandy wanted. There, in the parking lot of the Painters Mills Apartments, was the Indian. He was no longer at the corner, a reasonably safe distance from her, but right in the parking lot below her window. And he was sitting on the hood of her car looking up at her.

Sandy jumped back from the window. *Oh, my God!* she thought. *I'm not dreaming this! There's an Indian on the hood of my car!*

Without a moment's hesitation, she grabbed for the telephone sitting on the end table near the glassed doors to dial 911. It was then that she seemed to lock eyes with the Indian—phone in hand with a *9* and *1* already dialed. Though he was three floors down with glass and space between them, she could stare into his eyes as though he were there in the room with her.

She put the phone back into its cradle. Sandy's heart was beating hard and a cold sweat had reached her brow. Fear gripped her. The eyes gripped her.

And then, suddenly, a calm feeling came over her. She was no longer afraid. Stepping up to the window, she peered out into the gray morning at the Indian.

And she watched him disappear before her eyes.

††††††††††††††

Later that day, she sat with a close friend in a twenty-four-hour eatery on Reisterstown Road that served the best—and the greasiest—food available in the real world. Food of the gods, especially when one needed to unload tales of an Indian stalking.

"I swear to you," Sandy said to Samantha. "He was there, scarin' the hell out of me, and then, *poof*, he was gone. Well not, *poof*. He kinda melted away."

"I'm melting," Samantha croaked in a mimic of the Wicked Witch of the West.

"This is not funny," scolded Sandy. "Is this funny to you? I almost get kidnapped by an Indian and you just make jokes?"

"Kidnapped? Does that mean that you would have disappeared, too?" Samantha obviously thought Sandy had slipped over that hill of insanity.

"I'm being serious, Sam. I saw this guy."

Samantha relented. "Okay. So you saw an Indian who disappeared. People see ghosts all the time. Why not you?"

Sandy frowned. She'd not thought of this before. She'd seen a ghost. "But he wasn't like a ghost-ghost…I mean, he wasn't wispy and white and making weird sounds or anything…"

Samantha laughed. "You watch too much television. It's true that some ghosts do those very things, but you can have a ghost that looks as solid as you and me. There one minute—even talking to you—then gone the next. No ectoplasm, no ghostly shrieks, no *boo* in the face. Just gone."

Sandy was still frowning. "Ectoplasm…"

"Ghost goop. The residual stuff some ghosts leave behind."

"I didn't see any goop. Just the Indian. Then poof." Sandy paused. "But you know, at the end—after I got over being afraid, which by the way, I don't know why I got so calm—it was like it wasn't a ghost. It was like it was a ... friend." She knew Sam would scoff at this, but it had to be said. "It felt like it might be there to protect me..."

Sam just nodded and scooped more of the greasy scrambled eggs on to a wedge of toast. "Oh, okay. Not a ghost then. A spirit guide looking out for you."

Sandy hadn't touched her waffles and the whipped cream was melting down the sides of them. She dabbled at the food with her fork. "What? Spirit guide? And what is that?"

"Well, actually it could be a spirit guide—which I'm thinking because of you feeling protected there at the end and also because Puppers didn't do any of his characteristic barking mania kind of stuff—or...if there were Indians on that particular property way back when, it could be a residual haunting." She looked up at Sandy to realize that Sandy was waiting for more of an explanation. "A residual haunting is a ghost or ghostly scene that happens over and over again like a broken record kinda. They don't really know we're here and don't react to us. The just do their thing over and over." She took a bite. "I don't think your Indian is residual though, because he seemed to be interacting with you; giving you a calm feeling and sitting on your car and stuff. I mean how many cars are in that parking lot for him to have picked yours?"

Sandy was shaking her head in amazement. "How do you know all this stuff?"

Sam shrugged. "My grandmother told it to me. She's a sensitive. She knows all about this stuff. Mom thinks she's crazy half the time. But I believe her. She's got it right. I've seen stuff, too. I don't think about it most of the time."

"Really? You never mentioned it and it seems kinda big to keep secret," said Sandy.

"Not really. You'd be surprised the number of people who have supernatural—or as I like to say—super and natural—things happen to them and then they hide it, lie about it, or just dismiss it, so they don't either feel crazy or be accused of actually *being* crazy."

"Okay…" began Sandy. "If this Indian spirit guide is here to protect me…then, one, how is he going to do that? And two, what am I being protected from?" She was thinking of the snakehead she had bought last month and knew that, somehow, it figured into this new situation. Maybe it hadn't been a sucker purchase after all.

"Good questions all," said Sam, still heartily eating. "I think you'll know soon enough. Seriously, though, if you haven't seen him before and he is one of your spirit guides, you need to be on the look out for any issues that could be bad for you. A guide doesn't usually show himself so arbitrarily without purpose."

"Yikes. You make a good point. Maybe we could talk to your grandmother sometime…I'd like to understand this better."

"Sure, but enough of Indians and spirit guides. Don't you think you should tell me about Greg and your date tonight?"

Sandy just smiled.

†††††††††††††††

"Well, Puppers, I look sensational, if I do say so myself." Sandy was looking into the mirror at her reflection—new slacks, new top, make-up, and hair perfect. Puppers barked once in obvious approval. "Yeah, yeah," she said to the dog, stooping down to stroke him. "You'd think I looked great if I had two heads." Another bark.

She moved out into the living room, taking a quick glance out the glass doors and then stepped out onto the patio. She looked right and left and even leaned over the balcony to make sure there were no Indians in sight. All looked clear. Maybe the whole thing had been a fluke.

Back inside, she pulled the wine from the freezer—just the right chill. Two fragile glasses left to her from her grandmother's collection stood at the ready. *Okay,* she thought. *Wine, small talk, then off to dinner and the movies. The perfect evening. Great guy. Great me.*

But there was another thought trying to intrude, attempting to push its freaky little way into her brain. Something was not right. What was it? Was it the wine? Was it her? Was it Greg? It had to do with the Indian, of that she was sure, because she'd been glancing at the closed box containing the snakehead sitting stately on her book shelf all day. But then, ever since her friend's warning, she'd been on edge and her mind had gone wild with the possibilities of things to be protected from.

First it was traffic. It was horrendous on Reisterstown Road all the way down through Owings Mills—the road was alive. What if she had an accident? There were plenty of spots to be creamed. There by Reisterstown Road and just before Pleasant Hill Church, a blind spot over that hill always made her nervous.

Maybe her apartment was going to be robbed. It happened. Not that she had anything of super value, but Puppers was there and if anything happened to him, life would cease to exist.

Then there was her job. She was an executive secretary for a private investigative firm in Baltimore City not too far from Sinai Hospital in Pimlico. It wasn't the best of neighborhoods and she'd had many narrow misses with violence because of it.

Maybe it was Greg...though she didn't believe that. He was too nice.

Dismissing the intruding thoughts the best she could, she turned on the television, looking for a mindless comedy show to distract her. Greg would be there soon, and she could get on with her evening.

Greg's Turn

At one point, Greg had been excited about this first date with Sandy. She was a secretary for the detective agency that was providing guard dog services for the company he worked for. They'd met casually at her offices one afternoon when he was dropping off employee schedules for the next week. Seeing her one time made him the first to volunteer—well, if truth be told, the only volunteer—every week as the courier to run by the agency to give whatever had to be given.

She was *hot* and would certainly be a nice trophy to his *wall of women*. There was nothing sinister about the wall of women—it was just everyday snapshots taken of him with every one of the women he'd dated. It was a game to him now. How many could he get to fall for him before he moved on to the next one? No malice, no mistreatment, nothing freaky. Just him loving women. He always laughed when his friends called him a womanizer, but if the shoe fit...

And Sandy would be a perfect addition. Maybe the best one of all. Pretty as a picture, smart, witty. Maybe he'd date her a couple times before making that final move onward, just to keep her on the hook longer, to make the conquest sweeter. Ah, it would be a hard fall for her, but would be a great triumph for him. And his wall would be all the more beautiful.

He sighed. His friends also called him sick. And yes, it was true. But it was fun sick. Not sick-sick.

But that was at one point. He couldn't really think about that now.

He'd been seeing a strange Indian everyplace he looked ... and a really gross-looking, scary snake with a big mouth. The savage seemed to be staring at him, glaring, growling...just the meanest son of a gun he'd ever seen. And the snake just slithered around, looking like he was gonna strike at any minute. The first time he'd seen the Indian had been outside his office by his car when he'd gone that first time to drop off the schedules to Sandy's detective agency. He'd frowned and looked around to see if anyone else saw this strange sight, only to find no red man there when he looked back. Maybe he'd been imagining it. Maybe it was just stress. And he had after all watched that western on late-night TV the prior evening—there were Indians in that aplenty. He was just tired.

But then, every time he went to the detective agency, he'd see the Indian—and the snake was sunning itself on the blacktop of the parking lot. The man wasn't always around his car, though. Sometimes, he was on Northern Parkway, just standing there along the busy road watching him as he passed by. Or at the Plaza where he'd stop to get coffee, standing behind a potted plant. And one time, he was sitting on Sandy's car in the parking lot at the back of the building where she worked. It was maddening ...Or he was mad.

He'd look, and then always look away for an instant—it was like a natural instinct to look away from this..."thing"—and always when he looked back, the Indian and the snake would be gone.

One thing was for sure, whoever this Indian was, he was not a dancing, happy, peace-pipe kind of Indian. He was out for blood, painted in war paint, and brandishing a tomahawk. He was a warrior. The thing that worried Greg was that he truly felt that the blood this Indian wanted was his. This was a menacing character and one who should not be taken lightly.

Still, where did the warrior go so fast? And was he even there at all? Was Greg losing his mind? Was this a ghost Indian?

Greg shook the cobwebs of Indian and snake thoughts from his head. This was a first date and first dates held the ultimate of importance. One did not win a woman if that first date, first kiss, first *anything* else he could manage, didn't go well. He needed all his wits about him.

Still, his discomfort as he hopped onto I-95 from Towson was immense. It was as though his inner self knew that something was about to happen—something not so nice. The first stab of his consciousness washing over into reality came as he passed by the exit for Pikesville. The feeling was dread and there were now physical manifestations of fear and the fight-or-flight syndrome trying to take over. Every fiber in him wanted to take that ramp to Pikesville and flip right around and head back to his home near Eudowood. But he fought it and allowed the car to travel onward to 795 where he would exit to head out to Owings Mills and a beautiful evening with a scrumptious Sandy.

As he moved around the curve onto 795, he relaxed a bit. The traffic was lighter and some of his fear had fallen away. In fact, a lightness could be felt inside his car that was unusual. It was as though a foggy mass had invaded his brain with the ability to give gentle commands.

A soft whisper inside his head said, *Not her. Go back now. Before it is too late.*

He frowned and tried to dislodge the thought, but it would not go away. As he neared the Owings Mills exit on the right, he began to change lanes—Greg always drove in the fast lane. It was what he did. He looked up into his rearview mirror to make sure the coast was clear for a lane change.

Looking back at him in the reflection of the mirror, with a growling sneer on his face, was the Indian!

Greg tore his eyes from the mirror and screamed—a little girl scream that would send any of his friends into a torrent of laughter if they'd heard him. The car jerked out of control as he rapidly shifted across lanes and onto the shoulder, still going 65. Horns blared and cars swerved to miss him. He glanced back up into the mirror and the Indian was still there.

When he was finally able to skid to a stop, he threw open the driver-side door nearly having it ripped off by passing traffic. Greg ran to the side of the road and fell into a heap, his heart pounding, his body sweating, and fear sweeping through his mind. He stared back at his car, shaking.

It was then that the Baltimore County Police unit from the local Precinct 13 district pulled up behind his car. A young officer stepped out, crisp and formal.

"What seems to be the problem, sir," he asked.

Greg was stammering and staring, not at the cop, but towards the back seat of his car. "There's someone in the back of my car! I saw him in the rearview mirror!"

The officer immediately went on alert, his hand on his gun and his eyes focused on the car. He slowly approached the car and looked into the rear seat, then glanced into the front seat. His shoulders relaxed.

"No one there now, sir. Could he have run away? What did this person look like?" He was looking around him, but there were few places anyone could run to hide at the edge of the expressway.

Greg, without thinking, blurted it out and then was sorry. "It was an Indian! He's been following me for weeks!"

The officer blinked. "Have you had any alcoholic beverage today, sir? License and registration please."

It was a disastrous situation after that, with Greg looking quite the fool—he thanked God that he hadn't been drinking. Finally, knowing that it was his only recourse, other than having this cop cart him away to Spring Grove, he had to admit that it must have been his imagination. He'd been under a lot of stress lately. With that, the officer reluctantly sent him on his way—late for his date.

As the police car pulled away, Greg got back into the car with great trepidation. He looked in the back seat and then fiddled with the mirror, afraid that he would see the worse. But no Indian. This was nuts. And now he was angry.

He peeled off the shoulder cutting off oncoming traffic and gave rude gestures to those blowing their horns at him. Within a minute, he was at the exit and took the ramp that would lead him to Dolfield Road and the Painters Mill complex. Turning left, he headed back past Ritters Lane to the apartments. At the entrance to the development, he at first slammed on his brakes and then hit the gas shooting the car onto Millpaint Road. The Indian was on the corner. He was there, solid and angry, raising his tomahawk and doing some ritual dance. Greg rushed by him and a few buildings before looking back in his mirror.

He saw the Indian slowly fade into nothingness.

"Oh my God! Oh my God!" he was shouting inside his car. He'd seen a ghost! It had disappeared right before his eyes!

Quickly, he parked in front of Sandy's building and tore up the stairs to her apartment. Banging on the door, he practically fell inside as she opened it.

"You're not going to believe it!" he stammered. "I saw something!"

The Date

Sandy raised her eyebrows. He was nearly a half hour late and then shows up sweaty and crazy. Boy, could she pick 'em or what? Puppers was growling at him, too. That couldn't be good. The crazed eyes made good his timing, though—the story had to be good. She'd never seen a man so rattled.

"So what did you see?" she asked as she ushered him into the living room and pointed to the sofa. "Sit."

"I saw this Indian," he began. "And this rattlesnake..."

Sandy, sitting now, jumped to her feet, her eyes wide. "Where? Where did you see them?"

Confusion was as evident on Greg's face as the fear. "Where? Well everywhere...home, work, here..."

"Here, where?" she demanded.

"Right out front, at the apartment complex entrance. And the Indian disappeared right before my eyes, Sandy!"

Sandy was nodding and began to pace. Yes, this was her Indian and her snake alright. She was sure of it. So she wasn't the only one involved in this haunting. "Okay, tell me everything. I've seen him, too."

Greg quickly launched into a theatrical rendition of his Indian escapades making himself more the hero type than the frightened stalk-ee. But Sandy was not fooled; she'd seen the pale face and fear-stricken composure of the man when he'd arrived at her door. She moved to the patio windows and peeked out through the curtains. No one was there—rather no one who was not expected to be there. People came and went in the complex and this main drag through the development was well used.

After pouring Greg a glass of wine and doing her best to calm him, she decided to talk with him—in a limited way—about her own experiences and what her friend, Samantha, had told her about spirit guides. But she decided to not tell him that she thought this particular Indian and snake were there to protect her…from him. It had to be that, after all…

It was evident that the demeanor of the Brave was entirely different when he was interacting with Sandy than when he was visible to Greg. Though Sandy had been frightened at first, there was still a sense of purpose and a calming fog around her when he was around. Greg had described an entirely different experience. He was truly terrified and felt a discernable threat.

So, in Sandy's mind, the threat was not from the Indian or the snake, but from Greg—though she didn't understand how or why. He seemed harmless enough. But in the day of serial killers, kid-nappers, and perverted psychopaths, anything was possible.

She went to her bookshelf, pushed aside the box holding the likeness of the rattler, and pulled out a book. Holding the cover up for him to see, she said, "Look here. My friend, Samantha, lent this to me. It's about developing your psychic powers. It's about getting in touch with these things to find out what they are and what they want."

"Yeah, right! Like I wanna find that out!" Greg did not want to have anything to do with the book and leaned away from Sandy as she offered it to him.

"Don't be such a baby," she scolded, dropping the book on his lap. "It has a whole chapter about people seeing things like this."

The book was a traditional size paperback book, well-used with bent pages and no sharp edges.

Greg picked it up and stood up. He hadn't even opened the book, thereby separating the pages from the actual bulk of the paperback in his hands, when he yelped and immediately dropped it. His hand was bleeding profusely from the palm.

"I'm cut! I cut myself on the book!" He rushed to the kitchen and turned on the cold water, putting his hand beneath the stream of clear water. The water turned red with his blood pouring out of a wound in his hand that was much worse than a paper cut. It was a gash.

Sandy stood by him in the kitchen, wide eyed, as she watched the pinkish water swirling down to the drain. How could a paper cut cause this much blood? She reached for his hand to look at it.

The wound, centered in the palm of his hand, was nearly an inch long and had ragged edges. Blood swelled over those edges and down his wrist, even onto her own hand. She pushed it back under the water. "I'll go see if I can find some bandages and some peroxide."

As she went back into the living room on the way to the bathroom, she saw the book on the floor. Picking it up, she noticed one thing immediately. Not only were there no sharp edges on the book's pages, there was no blood. She turned the book over in her hands wondering what was going on. "No blood," she whispered. That wasn't possible if the book had truly cut him.

Once she'd bandaged Greg up, he was anxious to get away from her apartment. On edge and shaky, she couldn't tell whether it was the strange circumstances of his visit or that he felt an uncomfortable air about her. She certainly felt something odd in the place and kept scanning the room to make sure that they were alone. It did not feel like they were.

She watched him leave through the curtains that hung at the patio door. It didn't escape her that he sped up at the corner of Millpaint and squealed wheels onto Dolfield Road. The Indian on the corner watched him go and then turned back to look up at her. He raised one hand in the air to acknowledge her—a wave perhaps—and then…*he disappeared*.

††††††††††††††††

The next day, Greg stopped by Sandy's office to drop off the weekly schedule. He was distant and preoccupied.

"How's your hand?" she asked, noticing that the bandage she'd dressed him with was no longer on his hand.

He held up his hand to show her the palm. There was no gash. No angry mark. Nothing to show that anything had ever happened.

"It disappeared; blood, pain, gash, everything, as soon as I got home."

They just looked at each other, not knowing what to say.

Sandy never dated Greg after that, and in fact, he never asked her out again. And neither of them ever saw the Indian or the snake again, either. Well, except for the one in the box that sits on a bookshelf in her home to this day.

Epilog

Spirit guides have been talked about in Indian culture for a very long time, but I've only become closely involved with them—specifically animal totems and spirit guides—within the last two years or so. What I have learned, as an animal communicator (which turned out to be my ghostly calling—see my website at www.roseberrybooks.com to learn about my path into this world) is that everyone has an animal totem or spirit guide that stays with them throughout life. There are other animal spirits, however, that come to a person when the need arises. In this case, the snake came as a protective warning along with an Indian spirit guide. Most of us are not aware of these protecting beings that watch over us on a daily basis. But the more you look into the topic, the more aware you will be that these beings do exist and they are there to help—if called upon—and often, when not called upon, but when they perceive the need to be great.

Unfortunately, though these entities are always with us, most do not see them with our every-day eyes. How often have you heard of people (maybe even you) who have made a snap decision just in the nick of time and were uncertain where the epitome had come from? Yet it saved the day in some way! We often talk of these things as coincidences.

I specifically remember driving up I-83 one summer day near the Hunt Valley exit with a close friend—not during the horrendous rush hour, but in the middle of the afternoon. Something, and I hadn't a clue what, told me to change lanes—but not just change lanes, rather to drive on the shoulder of the road. *Right now!* I didn't think about or contemplate over the thought; I just did it. I swerved over to the shoulder.

At that very moment, a wheel barrel blew off the back of a pickup truck that was some distance ahead—right into the lane I'd been in seconds before. It bounced and then went into the fast lane. I was safe on the shoulder. (Luckily, there were no other cars in harm's way—just me.)

My friend asked me, "Oh my God! What made you go on the shoulder like that?!"

"I don't know," I said. "It was like someone was in my head who wasn't me. My mind said change lanes and do it NOW!"

At that time, I wasn't as aware of these beings. Oh, I had the little guardian angel pin that my mother gave me to wear, and one that hung from my visor, too, but I didn't really understand that those little pins represented real-live beings that interacted with me in a very personal way (from within my brain in this case) when the need was there.

…All that to say that spirit guides and guardian angels are real and help in tiny ways as well as big ways. Like protecting you from a wrong relationship. IF you listen.

Chapter Two

Murder on Antique Row

Gill's Flowers, Reisterstown

"I didn't go looking for it, but when I found it was there… it was hard to ignore."

— Christopher Balzano, *The Bridgewater Triangle*

Antique Row on Main Street (Route 140) running through Reisterstown is a wonderful place to stroll on a Saturday or Sunday afternoon, picking through used clothes and toys at a second-hand shop, getting some updated ski equipment, having some ice cream, browsing eclectic shops, or finding that perfect antique to compliment the home.

It wasn't always that way, though. Tragedy struck at one point. But let me start at the beginning.

Catherine was my grandmother. A wonderful woman; set in her ways, with very specific opinions about the world and the things that went on in it. A widow for some years, she lived on Main Street and ran a quaint flower shop from her home. The shop was located in the front room of her Main Street castle and sported a beautiful bay window filled with flowers and gardening paraphernalia fit for anyone wanting to begin or maintain the perfect garden. Sprinkled among the gardening items, were lovely little crocheted characters, animals that were knitted overtop dispensers for cleansers and such—decorative and creative displays of hominess. She had a knack for having the right gift for the person who had everything—right there in that little shop.

I spent many years in her home at the back of the shop and was intimately familiar with all the nooks and crannies that complimented a home that had the history of the 1800s flowing through it. From the second floor front of the building, one could look out at the traffic on Reisterstown Road—traffic that seemed to bring the road alive at all times of the day and night. I imagined what it was like to have horses and carriages instead of cars and trucks as I looked out that window as a little girl. There was a beautiful vanity made of wood with an antique mirror perched atop it in that front upstairs bedroom that drew me like a magnet when I was young. I'd sit there (when I wasn't being herded downstairs), but was careful not to touch the jewelry or potions that graced its top and I never looked into the drawers—that would be like interfering in my Grandmother's most secret places.

There was quite the family tradition going on at my Grandmother's house. Forever and a day brought the entire family together there to celebrate nearly every major holiday—and some not so major. I got to see all my cousins during these family times, and that was a treat because during the year, sometimes, there were just not enough days in the week or money in the bank to traipse all over Baltimore County for visits. Grandmother and the house on Main became a staple.

Not that I didn't cry the blues about going there on more than one occasion. At Christmas, I oftentimes didn't want to leave the cozy tree at my own house with the gifts galore—well galore being relative for middle-class folks in that time. But once there on Main Street, the days were always glorious and I look back fondly at these treasured moments in time.

But it wasn't only the house that was an important staple in life. Grandmother was as well. Thinking back, I find it so funny now how much I used to hate the Sunday rides. My grandfather was alive then, and my parents and both grandparents would stick me in the car and force me to see historic places, me carsick the entire time—I think they thought I was faking, but I wasn't. Gettysburg comes immediately to mind and the huge tower that one was expected to actually climb. I laugh now, because as a ghost hunter, Gettysburg is the primo trip and I clamor to go there every chance I get. It's a perfect example of not appreciating the moment and being sorry for it later. Still, I was young and kids are known for being cantankerous at times.

I was especially beholding to Grandmother because she let me get away with stuff that my mother would never allow. She fixed me foods that she new I loved. She hand-made me little gifts even into my adulthood. She was cool. And since I saw her so much more frequently than any other relative, there was a comfort level there. But I never thought about it. I took it for granted.

There was only one time in my whole life when she stung me. And she never knew it—though in her ghostly form, she does now. Harm was never meant and if she'd known that she'd devastated me over such a little thing, she would have scoffed and let me know in no uncertain terms that I needed to get over it. After all, it was a harmless comment.

It was in the 1980s, a time when women wore their hair in curly fashions. I had such a "do" and loved the ease of it. No maintenance whatsoever. And I liked the way I looked with the style. It did not go over well when she mentioned at a family gathering that it reminded her of a bird's nest. I'm laughing as I type this, and I can feel her here with me now, also laughing, but sorry that my feelings were hurt so by the judgment.

Premonitions?

Anyway, this story is not only about murder, but also of what any "Star Wars" fan would describe to you as a "disturbance in the force." Premonition or sharing of a moment—I'm not sure which—but there was a change in the flow of the world on that day in the 1980s that rocked my family's world.

At the time of this "disturbance," I was living in the "Oaks" in Parkville and I was just getting into the world of Tarot reading. I'd taken a regular pack of playing cards and wrote on them extensively, scribbling the meanings of each card on its front so that I wouldn't have to page through a book as I laid them out in a long-established Tarot spread. And I found that I was pretty good at it—which in later years would become part of my own psychic arsenal.

On this particular evening, I was practicing card readings with a friend and was showing her how it went, by laying out ten cards (in the classic spread called the Celtic Cross) to read my own future. Anyone who reads cards will usually tell you that reading for yourself is a confusing thing. You're so close to *you* that you can't interpret as well as might be expected. Or it's possible that what you see in the cards may not be what you want to interpret.

Whatever the case, this particular spread was predicting black-black-black things. Every negative card in the deck came up, hooked to every other negative card. I remember saying to my friend, "This whole reading is about death; I hope I don't get run over by a truck."

I pulled the cards back, reshuffled, and dealt them again. Same kind of reading. This was beyond coincidence, but at that time of my life, I still believed in coincidences. I didn't realize that all things happened for a reason. After about four tries, the whole card-reading idea became ... well, not fun. Too much negativity. I put them away.

The next day began as any other summer day. Well, no, that wasn't true. But I *tried* to make it start like any other day. The kids wanted to stay home this day from camp, and that was usually allowed as long as the oldest was there to watch them until I got home from work. Today, despite their protests—it was incredibly hot out and they didn't want to be at the camp that would be held outside in the heat at a local Parkville park—I made them go to camp. I usually drove them, but I couldn't that day. I don't know why I couldn't, but I just knew that I wasn't going to go to the park. I called my neighbor, who also had a child in camp, to come by and get my kids. She came; they went.

I was alone in the house. I paced about for a few minutes. Then I called work and told them I was sick—something I never did, because I loved the job and had ridiculously high work standards (thank you very much, Mother). I showered, dressed, put on makeup. I walked from room to room, sitting on the couch and then a dining room chair, opened the fridge (but didn't eat), I went upstairs, sat on the bed, back downstairs—over and over. I was waiting. But I didn't realize it. And I didn't know why.

The air in the house was heavy, not cold from air conditioning or hot from the summer heat, but heavy as though a presence was weighing down the molecules of air around me. My heart was beating continuously fast and it felt as though it was pounding hammer-like. I had a slight sweat on my brow and over my mouth.

What is this? I asked myself. *What is going on here?*

This odd internal and external behavior went on from about 8 a.m. that morning until 2 in the afternoon. Just after two, the phone rang.

My body went rigid and there were goose bumps covering my body. The hair on the back of my neck was standing up and I was remembering the card reading from the night before. I didn't want to answer the phone, but I knew I had to pick up the call before the fourth ring or it would go to answer mode. I knew I needed to get the call. And I knew it was bad.

This is why I'm here in this state, I said to myself as I picked up the phone.

I didn't even have to say hello when I picked up the receiver. My mother was already talking. "Your grandmother's been murdered. Get up there right away. Your father just left."

I felt as though someone punched me in the stomach when I put the phone down, but I allowed my subconscious brain to take over. I called and left a message for my significant other, then the neighbor who had my kids. I jumped into my car and headed for Reisterstown.

Death

What transpired afterwards was surreal to me—then and now. A clear picture is not available in my fogged mind. I arrived to a blocked-off Reisterstown Road. I abandoned my car, its driver's door wide open, in the middle of the street and ran (just like in the movies) to barrel through the line of police officers barring the way. They grabbed me. I identified myself—screaming. They sent me through and I was ushered into a home/business neighboring my grandmother's house by two detectives from the Homicide Division of Baltimore County Police.

To this day, I do not remember what happened to my car, who was in the room with me at this next-door location, who I talked to, or what happened following the incidents of the day. I believe that trauma blocked out the details. I do remember that a thick veil of sadness was around me and that it was neither mine nor those family members sharing that moment. It came from another source, an outside source.

This was also the case later on, going through the murder trial, as the killer was found and convicted—my grandmother now dead, minus the jar of change filled with pennies that she'd been robbed for. It was a nasty business that left me unable to watch any courtroom drama on television, read about a trial in the newspaper for any reason, or find solace in my heart for defense attorneys for over twenty-five years. Even now, I refuse to watch some of the most famous television shows that involve courtrooms. And I just hope that I don't get called for jury duty in my lifetime.

But Back to Spirits...

It was sometime after all the turmoil that the family decided to put Grandmother's house up for sale. Difficult to maintain and no one in my family having the financial resources to accomplish such a task, it went on the market. I wanted it desperately. But alas, I was unable to make that happen. Money was forever scarce.

It was bought, however, by a lovely lady whom the family knew. She remodeled it and turned it from a business/home to just a home. I was invited, along with my mother, to visit once it was completed. There was great trepidation, at first, for me. I wanted to go, but I was still missing my grandmother and afraid of my reactions. Yet, it would be my only chance to see the inside of the house again, I felt. (And that was true to this point.)

On the day my mother and I visited, it was sunny and bright. The buyer had done a lovely job with the place—Grandmother would have loved to have had the resources to bring it up to this notch. While my mother talked to the lady, I strolled into the living room. This was where her body had been found on that fateful day. I welled up. But then such a peaceful feeling fell over me, and the hairs on my neck stood up. I didn't realize then that this was her spirit communicating with me. This was pre-ghost days for me.

There was a stab of woe-is-me for losing someone without being able to say goodbye, but I left in one fairly stable piece. Arriving home, I sat on the little stool to the vanity that I'd been given to remember her by and went back to the time when I was a little girl, stealing moments at that mirror. And it was as if she was there beside me, choosing a piece of jewelry—or remarking about my bird's nest hair.

I moved that vanity with me to every new home for over twenty-five years, realizing little by little that she was no longer connected to it and that it was just a cheaply made, ply-board piece of furniture with no real value. It never fit in with my décor, but I used it religiously. Finally, a few years ago, I let go of it, as it was warped and looking worse with each passing year. You can still see the vanity stool though sitting stately in my house—and occupied mostly and regularly by my cat that has now claimed it as his own.

I still drive by the old house on Reisterstown Road—Main Street in that part of town—but it's no longer a house, but an office building. I've not gone back, but each time I drive by, there's a pale shadow in that upper front window where I'd sat with the vanity all those years ago. Was it Grandmother, or was it me I saw?

Epilog

Family spirits often leave premonitions, feelings, and impressions on those left behind. Again, these inklings of what's to come can surface from spirit guide/guardian angel interactions. They can also come from psychic phenomena available to each and every one of us through parts of the brain unused—okay, I don't know that for sure, but it's what I believe. Was I in touch with my grandmother at the time of her death? I don't know. Who was giving me the death readings while I was trying to understand the cards? That certainly had to be the guides. How did I know to make the appropriate arrangements for the children? The answers to these questions are all just outside my understanding and fall to conjecture.

In the months that followed my grandmother's death, I suffered greatly. I wasn't convinced of a world beyond, except for that very murky description provided by the church. I wanted to believe it, but who was there to verify it? It was then that I found a book entitled *We Don't Die*. I found it at the Parkville Library one day after I'd read every other book about death and dying that the library could provide me. The book was written by George Anderson, a psychic (pre John Edwards) who talked with those who had passed over—and some who'd gone in a violent way—in an effort to comfort the living. I remember reading that book at one setting (and it's not a short book). At the end, I put the book down and my grieving stage was over. It had that much impact on me. I've given that book as a gift many times over the years to others when loved ones died—no one seemed to have the same miraculous healing that I'd found from it (at least none that was told to me), but I know that this would be the beginning of my trek to learn about the "other side."

Chapter Three

The Night Visitor

Tollgate, Owings Mills

"That can't be good..."
— The Sheriff on Sci-Fi Channel's "Eureka"

James and Elsie lived near Owings Mills High School in the Tollgate area—a housing development located just off Reisterstown Road back when Owings Mills was very young and had little in the way of traffic and shopping centers. It was farmland at one time. But in this day and age, the area was a metropolis of activity and goings-on—some of them spooky.

Neither James nor Elsie thought much about paranormal occurrences in the world. Nothing had ever happened to them as far as they could remember. James liked a good scary ghost movie from time to time and had been known to spend most Saturday nights of earlier years in front of the television watching "Chiller" with his pre-teen daughter. But that had been many years ago, and now that he and Elsie were in their late seventies, staying up that late had its negative consequences on the next day. No movie was worth it.

There was a routine to be adhered to and Elsie was a stickler for that routine—James just went along with it because the things that Elsie did usually suited him just fine. In bed by nine, up by six. Once in a while, the television held them a little beyond that—*Dancing With the Stars* had Elsie addicted—but for the most part, they kept to the schedule.

Once in bed, both James and Elsie were the type who could go right to sleep. There was no rehashing of the day or chitchatting with an internal dialog or daydreams that most people seemed to have. They were there to sleep. And sleep they did.

But one night, things were different. They'd felt strange the whole day and wondered if they were coming down with something. The flu was going around—wasn't it always? They were forever extra careful when it came to "regular" sickness because, at their age, such maladies hit them so much harder than a younger person. And both had other health issues to contend with; diseases that many say are for the elderly. Of course, Elsie bah-humbugged that. It was all just a mean trick played on them by the universe. "Yes, youth is wasted on the young," you could always hear her say. Or, "If I knew then, what I know now, things would be different." They'd come to recognize that these were traditional things people said after they'd passed fifty, and both felt that the statements were ironically true.

But on this particular day, both James and Elsie had felt an eerie sensation buzzing about them all through the day. Several times Elsie had looked over her shoulder to see why in heaven's name James was so close to her, but always turned to find no one there. And James kept hearing Elsie call him—from a distance—but she'd never uttered a word his way. She'd been busy with her cleaning regiment. They found that often, during that first day, they'd glance at each other and each would see the other frowning about something or another that wasn't really there or hadn't really happened.

They dismissed it. No time for trivial nonsense about ghosts or any other strange things in their household. Elsie wouldn't have it and James thought it was all imagination. The fact was, they didn't think of the paranormal at all. There was a reason for everything and any thought of superstition, worlds or life beyond, was just not in their mindset.

That first night came as usual with the last commercial on the television and the regular quick trips to the bathroom before retiring. A storm was brewing outside, nothing big, but they could hear the rumble of thunder in the distance—surely headed their way.

James yawned. "I hope they got the cat in next door," he said. "It wouldn't be good to have him out there in the rain."

"Oh, I'm sure that cat will be just fine. Probably better than we are, if I know his antics. He'll just curl up someplace dry—under the porch or something—till it all blows over."

James merely nodded. The cat did seem to be industrious. They'd lost their cat many years ago, and though they both missed the company of cats and kittens in the home, they didn't miss the vet bills and other issues that came with them. It was just as easy these days to love and spoil the neighbor's cat.

"Ya know," remarked Elsie as she pulled the covers to her, "I feel kinda strange tonight. And I felt that way all day, too. There's like an electricity in the air—you know, like the hair on your arms standing up and goose bumps."

James shrugged. "Storms will do that."

"No," she said. "The weather just recently started to change. I've felt this all day. Like something's coming…"

"You watch too much TV."

"Don't you lay there and tell me I watch too much TV," she glared at him. "You watch the same amount as I do and you even watch the commercials."

He just laughed—knowing she was right. It was like hypnotism these days with the TV. They had you. They really did. The fact was some of the commercials were funnier than the shows.

"I do know what you mean, though," he said to her matter-of-factly. "I've felt odd today, too. Not sick exactly, but unsettled. And you're right; it's like something's coming." He paused. "What do you think it is?"

"I don't know," replied Elsie, "I just hope it doesn't wake me up once I get to sleep. I'll never get back to sleep if that happens."

They both sighed and turned out the lights.

†††††††††††††††

Sometime in the night, after they'd gone to sleep, something woke Elsie up. There were raindrops *tap, tap, tapping* on the roof and she could still hear a bit of thunder. Something, however, was not right. For one thing, the outside light was on. It was one of those motion lights and James had it rigged so that it only came on when something pretty big came within a certain distance of it. She didn't know how he managed to jury-rig it to do that, but he had once she complained that every time a leaf fell, the darn thing came on, blinding anyone within a mile of it. And...it was on now.

She reached over and shook James.

"James!" she whispered harshly. "James, wake up!"

He rolled over toward her and growled, "What? What time is it?"

"I don't know," she scolded as though he was a whining child, "but that back light is on."

James sat up in bed. "Crap. It's probably just a dog or a deer or something."

"Go see!" she instructed. "Go on now. Go see what it is."

James slid out of bed and stumbled towards the door of their bedroom.

"And don't put on the light," whispered Elsie. "You don't want anyone to see you looking at them!"

"Yeah, yeah," he grumbled.

James came back to the bedroom shortly thereafter and flipped on the light.

"Hey!" cried Elsie.

"Not to worry, dear," he said. "No one's out there. Must've been a deer from the woods looking to eat from our tomato plants again." He got back into bed. "Go back to sleep."

"Right," said Elsie. "Like that's gonna happen now." Getting back to sleep was difficult for her once she'd been awakened in such a manner. And she'd certainly pay for it the next day. She lay there with her eyes open, now accustomed to the dark. She could tell that James was also still awake because his breathing had not changed to that slow rhythm one has when asleep. That, and he wasn't snoring.

It was then that it seemed that the whole house became still in the night—no sounds of clocks ticking, no air conditioning motors, just silence. It was strange. Even stranger was that the rain had suddenly stopped and the world outside their home was still as well. That old saying about hearing a pin drop came to Elsie's mind.

Still, she lay there without moving, just listening to the silence. James was apparently doing the same.

Suddenly a small *tap, tap, tap* came at their bedroom window. Just three knocks and then silence.

In the darkness, James and Elsie could see each other sit up in bed. "What was that?" whispered Elsie.

"Knocking," replied James.

"Well, I know it was knocking, for Pete's sake! But *who* was knocking?" She glanced at the clock by the bed. "And at 2:22 in the morning!"

James slid out of bed again and peeked behind the curtain out into the driveway beyond their bedroom window. There was no one there of course. No car—other than their own—in the graveled carport. "Maybe it was Catchup..." he said, referring to the orange cat that lived next door.

"He wouldn't knock or tap like a person. And how would he reach the window to do it?" she remarked also getting out of bed. She began turning on lights.

"What are you doing?" James asked.

"Letting whoever's out there know that not only are we up, but they better hightail it back wherever they came from."

James just shook his head. "It was probably a tree branch blown down from the dogwood and hitting the window."

"Or a bird...it could've been a bird," offered Elsie.

"I'm sure it was nothing. Let's get back to bed."

Back in bed, both lay there listening for a while to see if any other strange noises caught their attention until finally, tired and strained from listening, both fell asleep.

Morning came quickly and both James and Elsie were tired. But there were things to do this day. Doctor's appointments, food shopping, a slew of errands. They moved through the day into the evening with little notice of anything strange. The odd feeling was still around them, like a current in the air, but neither of them spoke of it. Because it wasn't really there, was it?

That night, they went to bed via the same rituals and were quickly asleep. Elsie had been sure that they both would sleep like logs after the drama of the night before, but, again, something woke her up. It wasn't the backlight this time; she wasn't sure what it was. Glancing over at the clock, she saw that it was 2:21—and she watched the clock's face click over to 2:22.

James said, "Elsie? Are you awake?"

That startled her, especially since they'd both awakened at the same time and it really *was* the same time on the clock as the night before.

"Shhh," she whispered. "Feel that?"

And indeed he did. There was a buzzing in the air—voltage. And it seemed to hover about their beds and then it dissipated quite suddenly.

Tap, tap, tap on the window.

They both sat stock-still. No need for them to discuss hearing it. Those taps sounded thunderous in the silent room, though in reality they were just the clicking of ...something... on the glass window.

James whispered, "Was that noise from inside or outside the house?" His whisper was hoarse and shook a bit, as he moved again to look out the window.

"Don't look; don't go!" cried Elsie in a similar frantic whisper.

But that wouldn't hold James back. Again he looked and found nothing. And again, Elsie turned on all the lights in the house.

"Darn cat," said James, but Elsie could tell it was a half-hearted way to relieve her fears. She knew it wasn't the cat. But she didn't know who or what it was tapping on their window.

The next day, both James and Elsie went outside and investigated every inch of the area outside their window. They didn't watch *CSI* on television for nothing. There must be footprints or some kind of evidence of what was causing their strife at 2:22 two nights in a row. But alas, they found nothing.

"You just trampled all over the evidence, that's all that's happened here," remarked Elsie as she peered at the ground.

"I did not," he said. "Besides, it was wet out here last night and if there were tracks, they'd still be here in the soft ground. Nothing was here."

"Go ahead," she said, a clipped tone to her voice. "Just stand there and tell me it was imagination! I know you want to."

He stooped again to look at the ground. "I know it wasn't your imagination, Elsie. And it wasn't mine, either. I just don't know what it was. What taps on a window, but leaves no footprints in soft ground? Look at the tree; there are no branches that reach the window. And there's no debris that could have hit the window and fallen. Even the cat would've left a paw print or something, if he could even get to the window—which he can't." He stood up. "I just don't know."

Elsie did not like the answer, but knew it wasn't her husband's fault. Still, it scared her. And she'd been noticing something else, something that she hadn't told James. The electricity in the air had increased and it had stayed about her most of the day. Trying to chuck it up to imagination and being on edge due to the nighttime escapades of an intruder unknown, she'd ignored it. But she was very scared now. What was it? She could tell that James, too, was uncomfortable with the unknown.

But both of them forcefully dismissed it and went about their day. Inside however, they were distressed about the coming night. What would the night skies bring?

†††††††††††††††

At 2:21 they woke simultaneously, grabbing the other's hand in the darkness. The clock's faced clicked over to...*2:22*.

Tap, tap, tap.

This time the tapping was louder and more insistent. And unlike before, it repeated itself.

Tap, tap, tap.

They both hopped out of bed and tore to the window, throwing open the curtains.

This time they SAW something. A white foggy-looking mist was floating outside the window, hovering at eye level. It shifted and moved in front of them and then—*poof*—it was gone that quickly.

James and Elsie looked at each other with wide eyes. They'd both seen it and they both knew without a doubt that the mist was the "thing" tapping on their window.

Neither of them could sleep and this time, James joined Elsie in going around the house to turn on all the lights. They sat in the living room watching infomercials until the sun came up.

At just about 8 o'clock, the phone rang—an odd occurrence for so early in the day.

"Hello?" said Elsie into the receiver. "Uh-huh, Uh-huh. Yes, we'll be right there."

"What?" asked James when she'd hung up.

"My brother died last night. He'd been in the hospital for the last three days in and out of consciousness...and died last night just after 2 a.m. ..."

"I didn't know he was in that kind of shape; he was only going in for minor surgery..." said James.

Elsie sat down hard on a kitchen chair. "It was him, James. It was him tapping."

They went to the hospital, and were there to help with whatever arrangements needed to be made.

††††††††††††††

That night, Elsie set her clock for 2:15.

When the clock went off, neither of the two had been sleeping, both waiting for what would happen this night after Elsie's brother had died. They sat up in bed and waited for the clock to turn to 2:22. *Click*.

Suddenly, they both felt a peace settle over them and watched as a soft willowy mist came from the outside, through the wall, and into the bedroom. Both knew that it was the mist they'd seen the prior night.

It hovered in front of the bed and then slowly formed into the figure of a man—Elsie's brother. He was see-through, but she could still recognize his features.

"Paul..." she said softly.

The apparition merely nodded, smiled, and then... *disappeared*.

James and Elsie went to sleep after that and had the best rest they'd had in years. There was never a *tap, tap, tapping* at their window again.

Epilog

One thing that we hear all the time involves people who see family members at the time of or right after their deaths. Though science still seems to scoff at it, those who have seen or felt their loved ones at this most traumatic time don't really care what science thinks. One thing I can be often heard saying is: *Once you've had an experience, you don't care who believes and who doesn't. Popular opinion just doesn't matter anymore. It's now happened to you and you just know.*

This does not always happen with visual sight however. A tragedy touched my family as I was writing *Spooky York, Pennsylvania*; I lost a wonderful aunt to what lies beyond this mundane life we call reality. Fraught with remembrances of days long past, one often suffers in silence, for those in the "new life" haven't an idea of what such a person has meant over the years. But I found, happily, that my newfound ghostly experience level was a comfort. With certainty, I know that there's a place beyond that is a very loving and intelligent place for those who've chosen a life of good here on earth. Therefore, I was not totally surprised when my aunt visited me several times within a weeklong period after her passing.

How do I know this? My newly acquired (and often untested) paranormal training had prepared me for *knowing*. First, let me say that paranormal investigators are advised to always be aware of the internal thought process and how the mind throws thoughts or feelings randomly out for consideration when psychic phenomena is present. We are taught to spit out these thoughts no matter how odd they seem at the time.

Of course, during the work day, I tend not to spit out too much of this thinking—the people in my office already think I'm *out there* with, though they are mostly polite about it. But, while I don't call out my "knowings" all the time or use the fanfare of bells and whistles, I do make special note of these "perks."

After my aunt's death, I was *forced* to take special note—she would have it no other way. And interestingly enough, I was writing this book about York—a place she'd spent the last of her life (specifically in the Hanover area) after moving from Baltimore some years prior. She made herself known very well to me after her passing.

I would be working heartily at my desk, full focus on the project before me, and a forceful thought of her would overtake my concentration—and the overhead lights would begin to flash in an annoying flicker light show. The first ten times this happened, I noted it, and then pushed it from my mind. (*Darn lights. Guess I'll need to replace the bulbs*.) Though I'm learning the ghostly ropes, I find that I still question my perception of things just like a "normal" person—it's my imagination, I'm under stress, the lights are just those forever bothersome, blinking-for-no-darn-reason, overhead monstrous florescent lights.

I do believe that ghosts (a passed loved one in this case) have incredibly good senses of humor—especially if that were the case in life. My aunt had a dry humor. I'd heard her giggle a time or two over the years, but mostly a very calm dry wit defined her personality. And now, she was exercising that wit—she'd started to play with me to let me know that she was about.

Now I have no absolute proof of what I'm about to tell you, other than I *know* that it happened exactly as I'm reporting it and that it wasn't me just being careless, imaginative, or any other negatively-charged criticism you might have to offer. Feel free to *not* believe me, but it doesn't matter. Things happened and I know what I know.

As an editor, I work with many other authors on delightfully exciting ghost books—it's a true passion. I was working on such a project for one of my fellow authors. There is a process to putting a book together for publication, and during that process, I interact with designers and other important people to get the job done—

hopefully right. The designers here are angelic. They put up with a lot. And for those of you old enough to remember Lurch from the original "Adams Family" television show, I think that these young men and women just shake their heads and grumble at me in the Lurch fashion as they are forced to entertain ghostly projects that I'm involved with. It's a wonder they don't have large crosses at their desks warding me away. (No wait, that's for vampires...)

Anyway, I am responsible for looking at book layouts prior to the author seeing them and for checking important technical facts and numbers—namely the ISBN number, basically an identification number that lives with a book forevermore once published. I conduct this task every single time I work with a book by checking the copyright page provided to me by the designer on the final layouts. Every single time—no deviation. I look at the copyright page and check the number. This time was no different.

Some time after I'd sent the book back to the designer, he returned to me wondering where in the world I'd found the ISBN number that was listed on the form I'd submitted. The number I'd used came from a book that was published nearly a year before—a book about levitation, saints, and the reality of paranormal events through the ages (*Human Levitation* by Preston Dennett). I was mystified. I'm fairly certain that the designer thought I was just crazy and careless. But I swear...that's not the number I'd okayed... why would I go back in time to pull a number from an old book that was down in the warehouse (far from my desk) and put it on a new book? Such an undertaking would take much time and great effort on my part.

But the story does not end there. The very next ghost book I worked with that day, the same thing happened. By now, I may as well have played the music for the "Twilight Zone" in my office—that, or the theme from "One Flew Over a Cuckoo's Nest." I couldn't explain it, but I *knew* that I'd checked these two books correctly. (I can still see the, "Yeah, sure you did," in the designer's eyes.)

Immediately after the designer left my office—on both occasions—a picture of my aunt popped into my head, her wry smile twinkling in her eyes. I shook it off.

But she wasn't done with me. Tina is the president of the line that handles the ghost books and my mentor in publishing. I respect her greatly. I would *not* steal her house keys—I swear this to you. Yet, her house keys found their way inside my purse one afternoon. I know with all my heart that I did not take her keys! Still, there they were in my purse. My aunt popped into my head when I found them initially as I sat in my car. (Tina was locked out of her house.) I shook it off.

Still another poor designer's car battery went dead—parked next to mine in the office parking lot. Dead as dead could be. Now I don't think that my ghostly interactions had anything to do with the battery drain (though there are those who've mentioned that possibility). But the flasher lights flashed when I walked up to the car and stopped when I went away—even though the battery was so dead that a jump would not start the engine. The lights flashed at me a couple times—enough to have the publisher mention it, wondering if my ghosts were around. My aunt popped into my head. This time I mentioned it out loud. "It's probably my aunt." No one listened (remember, they think I'm bizarre).

I use a backpack type purse. I watched the strap pop off while it was sitting on my desk, untouched. My aunt again. I shook it off. You'd think I'd learn. But this is how it goes when you doubt yourself or your ability to touch those beyond.

At home, things were occurring as well—one of the most interesting was the jelly jar lid incident. (Silly, silly things!) I'd made a peanut butter and jelly sandwich for my lunch at work the next day. Cleaning up, I noticed that the lid to the jelly jar was missing. I looked everywhere. I cleaned the entire countertop, looked in the trashcan, and went over the kitchen with a passion. No lid. Finally, aggravated and tired of looking, I put foil around the jar's opening and put it back in the fridge. Telling my husband about it when he got home, he was mystified—and he absolutely hates a mystery. He tore the kitchen apart. (After all, *no* one should ever put a jar without a lid in the refrigerator.) He found nothing. We left the room.

About a half hour later, I walked back out into the kitchen; and there was the lid sitting on the counter—all alone with nothing around it, like it had been there forever. I got a snapshot in my mind of my aunt. (I smiled, but shook it off. Well, to be honest, I made a big deal about it, but no sense wiping up spilled jelly now.)

The smoke alarm had been driving me nuts, as well—at 3 a.m. in the morning. One beep. Ten minutes later...another beep. It was just enough to wake me up and then...it would stop. The battery in the alarm was new and the other smoke alarms in the house were silent. It happened so often that I pulled it off the wall that week. (I refused to entertain any thought of *anyone* at 3 in the morning, so no shaking off to do—just grumbling.) Not to worry, though. We have two other smoke detectors that are hard-wired and they are working fine—that is, working but not *waking* me at 3 a.m. for no reason.

That next morning, I made a formal request—out loud—to my aunt. I acknowledged that she was visiting, told her that I'd miss her terribly, and talked with her about some personal things. Then I asked that she not do these little things that kept me on edge and that made others think I was crazy. (All I felt was calmness.)

When I went out to my car that morning to go to work, it was breezy. But on my windshield, despite the wind, was the smallest little yellow flower that I'd ever seen facing me right as I looked out my driver-side windshield. I had a flash of her in my mind and a very warm feeling.

That was one week following her death, and aside from the flashing lights in my office as I typed this story, and the small shivers that I felt that told me she was reading over my shoulder, I've not heard from her since.

Relatives and loved ones who pass do visit us.

Chapter Four

Shooting down 911

Kenilworth Drive, Towson

"...sometimes two events or incidents can happen at the same time, even thought they're apparently logically unrelated, yet the combination of those two events produces a useful outcome."

— Geof Gray-Cobb, *Twist Your Fate*

Way back when (in the 1970s), the Baltimore County Police Headquarters used to be located on Kennilworth Drive at the corner of Bosley Avenue in Towson. The prison located there now was just a parking lot for everyone who had business at headquarters—detectives and police dispatchers mostly. The people who worked in the Communications Department worked as teams on three separate swing shifts. Therefore, they did everything together for roughly 48 hours a week—daytime, nighttime, holidays, weekends. This also included psychic encounters. But I'm getting ahead of myself.

Chelsea and Chase-Anne worked on Shift 2 along with about fifteen other people—a combination of police officers and civilians all coming together for the betterment of the whole police department and the county in general. Well, at least that's what people said out loud. It was a hard job, filled with aggression, stress, and personality quirks—much like any other work environment, if you think about it. It was a place, however, where close-knit relationships were developed and a family atmosphere maintained—good, bad, or paranormal.

The two young women became close quickly and found that they both had a penchant for psychics, Tarot, and any other classification linked to the "other world." In fact, Chase-Anne had a friend who had a friend who knew firsthand of a fantastically good psychic living right in the heart of Baltimore City on Cathedral Street. Furthermore, he was willing to come to one of their homes for something that was called a Psychic Party. Now this was right up their alley. So, they invited a small group of people (no one else from the police shift at first) to the first psychic party to check out their futures. They had a need to know who would be their future husbands and what was in store for them beyond their stress-filled days at the department.

The Saturday night of the party was electric. Everyone—all females—was excited to meet this much talked about psychic,

Jamie-Jon, who would change their lives forever. Or not. Either way, there was wine, and cheese, and potato chips; enough to feed an army of partygoers or at least the number of people that would cram into the Rosedale apartment of Chase-Anne's friend. (Worst-case scenario, if the party was a bust, they could go to the Golden Ring Mall.)

Chase-Anne was familiar with what was to happen at this gathering as her friend had been to such a function many times and had been urging her to go to one for some time. Chelsea, however, hadn't a clue as to what to expect. She found that she was running through her mind exactly what questions she wanted the psychic to answer that evening.

When Jamie-Jon arrived, he was not what either woman had expected. He was elderly—though at that time, for the ladies in their twenty-something lives, old was certainly relative and began at thirty-five. This man seemed to be in his late forties—early one hundreds in their eyes. He was on the heavy side and had piercing eyes. He came in quietly and looked at everyone individually and then centered in on Chelsea.

"Why are you so frigid in bed?" he asked her.

Chelsea was taken aback and frankly infuriated that he'd have the audacity to even question her about such a thing—let alone say it out loud in public. And besides, it wasn't true. (Was it?) She laughed and stammered something out that made no sense.

He just headed toward the kitchen, mumbling, "I only tell it like I 'see' it..."

The outburst, of course, brought forth much laughter and chiding, making Chelsea sorry that she'd come. But she was a trooper and played along with the crowd.

The "party" soon began. It consisted of ten women situated about the living room in a rough circle of furniture—couch, love seat, and dining room chairs. Jamie-Jon, with just a glass of water at his side and a notepad in his lap, began a well-used opening speech. He told them briefly that a spirit guide helped him with his predictions by giving him signs, symbols, pictures, and sometimes words. These things he then interpreted. There would be times when he would ask them questions and they were to answer truthfully. He said that he would know immediately if any of them were lying and would then discontinue the reading. They were then advised that he would say only the truth about the things he saw and would not lie or honey-coat a truth to spare feelings. Then he went around the circle asking each person individually if they were able to accept the truths he told. Everyone said yes, of course, but Chelsea wasn't sure if that had been such a good idea.

The readings started. There was no privacy. The readings were given aloud in a group session with others listening to any dirty laundry that Jamie-Jon felt compelled to dredge up. And there was plenty. But the laughing stopped and no one made fun of anyone else, least they be next on the chopping block.

Jamie-Jon was amazing. He honed in on issues that were so deep and secret for some of the people that one could hear a mosquito circle in the air. He spent about twenty minutes with each person, writing down, in terrible handwriting, key things he saw so that he could offer that to the person once the reading was over.

Chase-Anne was disappointed in her reading. He'd told her very little—it was as though she had no life, she told Chelsea later. It was strange how he could not read for certain people, but could talk to the soul of others.

When it was Chelsea's turn, she sat quietly as he went into his trance-like state and then opened his eyes. She learned that her car had a loose wire that would cause her difficulty (and upon checking later, it did), she would be getting a promotion, but would not be happy with it (which she did, but with no more money), and many other incidental things—mostly all of which came true. He then narrowed in again on her romantic life, spilling its contents on the floor for all to see. The bottom line was this thinking that she was a cold lover. She listened and answered his questions, though her face burned with embarrassment. Her thoughts, once it was over, were that she'd paid twenty dollars to be humiliated.

Still, in weeks to come, she found that he was fifty-fifty on being correct. And those were interesting numbers. (Thank God she'd not had an accident with a green car…though she made sure for all the years after that, even though green was her favorite color, never buy a green car—fifty-fifty odds were just too high to risk it. Jamie-Jon had told them that his predictions usually came true within a two-year time frame, but she'd found that the reach was oftentimes beyond that.)

Back at the police department, Chase-Anne had the place abuzz about how much fun they'd had—and how weird it was. Eventually, the two ladies began recruiting one after another of Shift 2 workers to participate in one of these psychic parties and one was planned where everyone on the shift was invited. Not everyone came, but many did.

Jamie-Jon never varied his routine, so the night that he came to the apartment in Towson along Loch Raven Boulevard not very far from headquarters, most of the group was familiar with his style and also knew that a deep-dark secret or two might be harped upon—they'd been warned. But remember, the shift was as close as family and this wasn't a big concern. So the night progressed and each person was put under the spotlight to squirm. It was fun.

Until the very end.

Before Jamie-Jon finished up for the night, he became very somber. "I have something I need to tell all of you—I've seen it more than once tonight. And it affects most of you here. You all did say that you wanted the truth."

Everyone nodded, but became wary. The man was good at what he did and had touched everyone in some personal fashion that evening. What could make him so uncomfortable?

Jamie-Jon took a breath and said, "I will tell you the picture I saw and then you must interpret it. I saw a long room, lined on one side with windows that you all could see out of, but that no one could see inside. There was a big long table in the room—taking up much of the room's space and many were sitting around the table talking on the telephones there." He stopped and pulled out a handkerchief to mop his forehead. "Then right after that, I saw another picture. The windows had been shot out with machine guns. Glass was everywhere. Things were in a shamble. And there were dead, bloody bodies scattered on the floor. Some of you were there on that floor."

The room was silent and everyone was just looking around at each other with wide eyes. This was a scary premise. The psychic had described the communications telephone room at police dispatch where they all worked. The room was long and rectangular with an equally long table within. Telephones were spaced along the table on both sides. The windows, lining the one side of the room and visible from Bosley Avenue, were bullet proof (supposedly) and covered with material that allowed one to see out, but no one to see in. There was no question in anyone's mind that the room that Jamie-Jon had described was the place they'd called home away from home forty-eight plus hours a week.

The more macho of the attendees—the police officers—began to chuff. Jokes and rude remarks started to flow from their mouths in a protesting way that merely amplified their discomfort at what sounded to be a possibility.

After all, everyone knew from the stories that were offered from the others in their group who'd attended these parties before that Jamie-Joe had a reasonable rate of success—even as high as seventy percent for some people. The party ended on a down note instead of one of excitement and fun.

In the weeks after, most of the attendees consoled each other by rationalizing Jamie-Joe's prediction. It was hogwash (although stated in a much more colorful way), ridiculous (things like that didn't happen in the real world), and simply dumb (because there was no such thing as psychic phenomena anyway). Chase-Anne and Chelsea sat on the fence in all the conversations. They knew too well that there was a possibility of roughly fifty-fifty that there could be threats of a terrorist nature there at police headquarters. Not only was the entire detective squad located on premises, but the communications department housing police dispatch, the telephone room, and teletype interface that serviced the entire county were also in the building.

For two years, they would have to sit on pins and needles, keeping a close eye on the telephone room windows and being more cautious than they already were when entering the building. Eyes and ears open. Interestingly enough, you would think that this would be the case anyway in a high-security facility. But there was usually an air of safety—and family as mentioned before—once a person was buzzed inside the locked doors. Locked away from the outside, one tended to develop a calm that allowed high efficiency on the job.

In short fare, most of the group forgot or disregarded Jamie-Jon's prediction over the following months when nothing out of the ordinary happened. Oh, the crime in the county was still occurring, but it was out there in the masses and not within the confines of the safe and secure headquarters building. Everyone relaxed. No one would be shot "today."

The Truth—or Untruth—of the Prediction

Psychic phenomenon is strange, and when considered by an individual, each person takes away with them what truth—or untruths—seem to fit their own realities. It's a matter of interpretation. For example—and this is a true example from one of Jamie-

Jon's sessions: If Jamie-Jon (or any other psychic) sees an image or receives an impression, the interpretation he tells the group is his alone. Each person listening to that vision/interpretation then places their own understanding and analysis on the statements. Once, Jamie-Jon told Chelsea that he saw a man at the top of a rope who was swinging wildly and this man seemed to be hanging on for dear life. He asked Chelsea, "Who is this man?" Chelsea replied that this man was her boyfriend and that he was struggling to hang on because his ex-wife continued to try to take his children from him and he didn't know what to do. Chase-Anne, her close friend, piped up to say: "Maybe it's not him, but your boyfriend's son, who is struggling to hang on because of all the problems at school." (He'd been having issues with a bully.) The boyfriend, who was sitting quietly said, "No, I think it's me, all right, but I'm struggling to hang on because my boss is giving me real grief at work..."

All this speculation got everyone thinking and everyone had a different variation of what this could mean. It's just like the old comparison of a rose—in a vase or on a coffin. People think of different things when they look at the same picture. And it's usually only after-the-fact, that the prediction becomes clear.

The problem when dealing with psychics in many cases is that some of the things they see are literal and other things may be symbolic. Figuring that out can be frustrating.

Chelsea found out, once her boyfriend dumped her for another woman, that the man on the rope was him and that he had been trying to hang onto his sanity because he was leading a double life—two women, two engagements. Furthermore, she later found out that one of the reasons she was dumped was that he felt she was too cold in their romantic life compared to the other woman. This prediction was literal.

Ah, but the police department telephone room. What of *this* prediction? It was not literally shot up and people were not splattered across the floor in any true sense. What happened was this:

Baltimore County brought in a new experimental first-of-its-kind 911 emergency system, built underneath the courthouse area in the heart of Towson in the late 1970s (circa 1979). The telephone room and all of police dispatch were gutted, dismantled, torn down. People in communications were stressed to the max—this new system was intimidating and some felt they did not have the ability to learn such a complex thing. It was felt that jobs would be lost and people would be dumped after years of faithful service if they didn't come up to par with the new developments. Lives would be destroyed. The consensus was for many that they'd been shot down in their prime and their comfortable surroundings (the telephone room and dispatch areas) were blown apart as though a bomb had been planted in their lives.

The entire prediction was figurative. But it was true.

Epilog

Jamie-Jon stayed in the lives of Chase-Anne and Chelsea for many years to follow. He, for a while, took a position at the old Palmer House restaurant downtown, reading Tarot cards and giving psychic readings. The ladies went at least twice a year to see him and attended parties whenever they could. Mostly, his predictions were fun. But Chelsea is still waiting to be killed in Florida as he advised her in readings taking place during three consecutive years. She is staying put in Mid-Atlantic region—or anyplace else in the world besides Florida. Fifty-fifty are still good (or bad) odds.

The thing to remember when talking with psychics is that there are two side issues to consider. The first is that of interpretation. One person's interpretation of a particular thing might not be the same as another's. The questions of literal or symbolic must always be considered. Additionally, predictions even if "right on," tend to only be true if the circumstances surrounding the issue remain exactly the same. If you do something that changes the climate of the situation, then the prediction may no longer be valid—or possibly could be off-kilter somehow. For example, if it's predicted that you'll have an accident while in a green car, and then you never get into a green car again, maybe that accident will come in another fashion, because you've changed your pattern. These things can be maddening if you're trying to take predictions seriously. Therefore, it's best never to live your life based on predictions or psychic readings. They are meant as guidance and helpful nudges, and major life decisions should be weighed in other manners and not made specifically because a psychic told you the outcome of a particular situation. This is difficult to swallow at times when you find a psychic that has told you specific things that have come to pass. But any psychic worth his or her salt will caution you that these things are not always black and white. The gray is very dominant and must be looked at carefully.

Chapter Five

Shadow People and Psychic Phenomena

Perring Parkway Apartments

(behind the Perring Parkway Shopping Center at Perring Parkway and Joppa Roads)

"God does not send us misery —we make our own."

— Dr. Hans Holzer, *The Spirit Connection*

Marty

Not all people were normal. Marty knew that and had known it since he'd gotten back from Vietnam. And he was the worse. In 'Nam, it had been bad—the worst days of his life. Because he was short and small of stature, he was forced to be one of the tunnel rats that had to crawl down into holes in the ground, dug by the enemy as hiding places for the Viet Cong. It was terrifying to go down into one of those jungle holes; they were barely big enough to squeeze through, his firearm with bayonet pushed along in front of him in case the worst happened—which was what he was looking for. Killing and crawling. It was the most frightening thing in the world and something that marked him and his psyche for an eternity. He'd never gotten over it. There were days that not one thought of those jungle hideaways came to his mind. On those days, he was just like anyone else. But then, when he least expected it, a shot from that time would explode in his mind, taking him back to the atrocities of war.

But he did learn to cope with the horror while he was over there in the jungles amongst the enemy. While there in the rice paddies, he'd met a religious Indian priest who taught him the fine art of meditation. Marty learned to leave his body when the worst of things—like finding a murderous enemy in a hole—happened to him. His body could take the measures needed to safeguard himself and his unit, and get him out of the hole in one piece; and all the while, his mind could push the incident away and take him to another place of calm, beauty, and joy. Of course, there were drugs, too, that helped—mostly pot, but it absolutely helped him maintain that place of sanctuary. He grew to love those places in his mind and systematically exorcised the real world around him.

When he got back in the states to his home in the Perring Parkway area of Baltimore County, things were not easy for him, though. It was increasingly more difficult to control the spurts of rage and fear, and also the sanctuary that would drop him out of his body in an instance without his desire to do so. He'd be involved in daily things and just go into a trance, forgetting that he was in the middle of a conversation, or in the shower, or working a job. Counseling didn't help much. Drugs (the prescription kind, now that he was home) only served to act as a crutch and he was always going on and off them. He didn't want to be addicted to the medications. He wanted to be in control. Yet he lacked the mental fortitude to face the problem.

And there was something else. A side effect came along with the meditation skills he'd developed in Vietnam. He'd become psychic—or psycho. That was the scariest thing. It was totally uncontrollable and dealt only with him and his internal strife. He couldn't tell others what was in their futures or even find the proverbial lost cat. Instead, he was given snippets about his own life—he just *knew* things. It was maddening and he did every single thing he could to dismiss it, ignore it, and deny it. But never did he try to understand it.

This skill, as some called it, always brought along memories of the times in the jungles and he did not want those memories. Ever. So wanting to fix the problem became still another problem.

Of course, life always has other plans. There were things out of his control when it came to this "knowing" he'd developed as a side effect. The telephone was the most frequent intrusion of the ability. He always knew before it would ring that it was about to. And he'd always know who was on the other end and what they wanted—if they wanted something from him. But that wasn't so bad; and if that were all it was, he would not have been so traumatized all the time. The problems revolved around his dreams. Well, if he were honest, they weren't dreams—at least not the sleeping kind. These were the "awake" kind. He felt like he was in a dream state and the visions had dream qualities about them, but he was awake. At least, he *thought* he was awake. One could never be sure anymore.

At any rate, things were worse now. There was this woman. (Wasn't there always a woman?) And he really liked her. And she really liked that paranormal who-do voodoo weirdo stuff. She wanted him to embrace these "gifts" as she called them.

He'd made the mistake one day of announcing the caller on the phone and what they wanted *BEFORE* the phone rang. She just raised her pretty eyebrows and asked how he'd known that. At the time, he just shrugged and told her it was just something he could do. As far as he was concerned, that was the end of story.

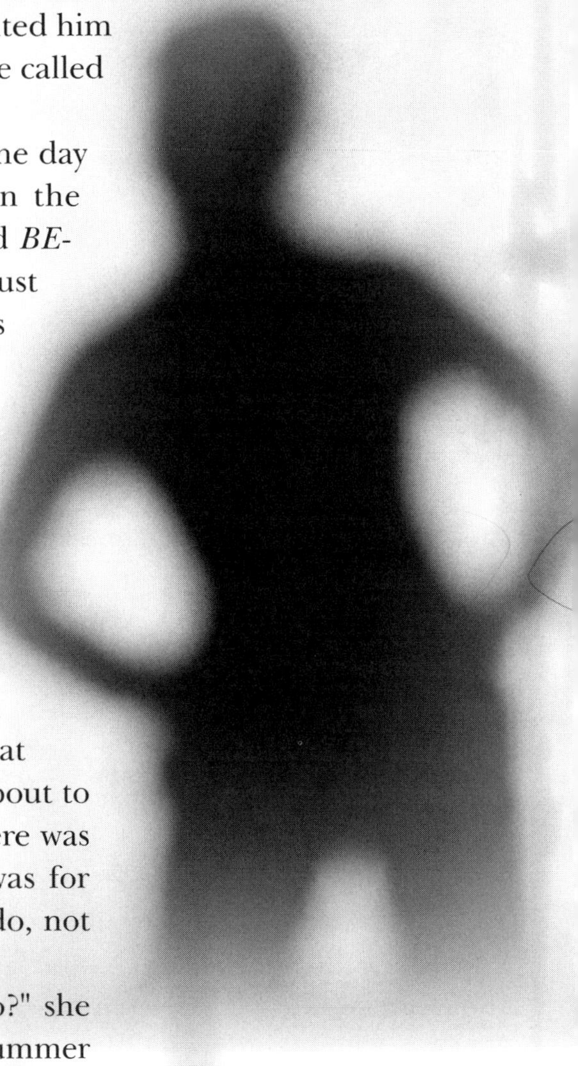

But not for her. Oh no. Sara had grabbed hold of that like a Pit Bull tearing at a T-bone steak. She wasn't about to let go—no matter what. There was hunger in her eyes and it was for him—rather what he could do, not specifically for him.

"So what else can you do?" she asked, leaning forward that summer afternoon. "You're psychic if you can do that."

"I'm not psychic," Marty defended and shrugged. "It's no big deal. Everybody can do it from time to time. I do it just a bit more often."

"Well," she began, "it's true that everyone is psychic to some degree—we just don't all use that portion of our brains is what I believe. I've been trying for the longest time to exercise mine, but no go, if you know what I mean."

Marty nodded and then got up to get them sodas.

"Do you have any playing cards?" she asked innocently.

Phew, thought Marty. That was that. She was done with the psychic questions. He had a deck of well-used cards because playing Pitch was a favorite thing for him and his brother to do when they got together at his mother's house. It passed the time.

Marty's trouble was that not only didn't he understand psychic phenomena, he didn't understand women, either. Sara had not left the subject go—she'd merely diverted it to something that would appear to be harmless play.

Marty handed her the deck of cards and she began to shuffle them. After a minute or so, she laid the deck face down on the table and then pulled one, holding it so only she could see what the card was.

"Okay," she said to Marty, "tell me what card I'm holding."

Marty narrowed, and then rolled his eyes. "You've got to be kidding. I can't do that."

"Sure you can," she announced. "Come on, Marty; just try. For me."

Marty took a deep breath and then took that same breath back in quickly. There above Sara's head was a shadow in the shape of a person from the waist up. It just hovered at the back of Sara's shoulder. Marty couldn't move, couldn't talk, couldn't breathe. He could only stare at the shadow. It shifted and churned behind her, not taking a specific shape of the man for more than a second before sinking back into a fogged cloudy black image. Then back into the shadow person.

Sara looked back over her shoulder to see what had spooked her friend, but there was nothing there. She turned back. "Come *on*, Marty! What card do I have?"

He couldn't believe that she could not see the same shadow that he could see, because it was right behind her, nearly touching her hair with its dark sustenance. It was then he noticed that the shadow was not entirely dark. In the center of it, in the area where a hand might be located if a person were standing there holding something, he could see a small gray glow. The glow then turned into a solid likeness of a playing card—the Queen of Hearts.

Marty looked at the card that the shadow was holding and then down at Sara, who was for all intents and purposes trying to think hard about the card in her hand in an effort to forecast it to his mind. He shook his head, knowing he didn't need her to push the thought his way. He could just take it from her.

"Queen of Hearts," he said without ceremony.

"Oh, my, God! That's right!"

She pulled another card.

He glanced up at the shadow. It was now holding the nine of spades.

"Nine of spades."

She pulled another and another until they'd gone through the whole deck. He'd identified fifty-two out of *fifty-two* cards.

The shadow seemed to spin in some elated fashion behind Sara's back. Marty just tilted his head back and forth, like a dog trying to understand a human. This was a first for him, and such an odd thing. A shadow person. Should he tell Sara? he wondered. And then answered himself right away. No. That would not be a smart thing to do.

"Here," he said taking the deck from her and shuffling it. "Now you try."

"But I'm not psychic; I can't do it," she said.

"Try," was all he said as he pulled the first card. He looked at the ten of diamonds in his hand and then projected the thought to her.

"Ten of Diamonds?" she asked tentatively.

He showed her the card and watched her eyes grow wide. The shadow behind her seemed to dance. He pulled another, sent the message, and she got it. Again, fifty-two out of fifty-two.

So... He was able to read minds and also project thoughts into other people's minds. This was handy. Some of his prior fear of the unknown began to dissipate. Psychic phenomena had value.

Over the next weeks, he noted that the shadow was around his Perring Parkway apartment most of the time, but he didn't fear it; he just wondered about it. More and more experiments were taking place with Sara, as her appetite was ferocious when it came to this stuff and just the fact that she was an integral part in the study of his abilities made her even more interested.

The latest experiment had him thinking of a certain song on the radio at exactly 10 p.m. that evening and then projecting it across the county from his location in Perring Parkway to Sara's apartment in Town and Country Woodlawn. Then, he was to write the song down on paper and seal it in an envelope. She was to do the same with what she received in her mind. A mutual friend would then open both envelopes the next day at the same time to see if they could communicate over distances. And sure enough, they could.

Still another time, without provocation from Sara, he had a strange vision. He'd been taking a nap on the living room sofa of his apartment—at least he'd thought he was asleep—when he suddenly saw his television switch on. Only there were no scheduled programs showing. Instead, he saw himself at the bottom of an empty swimming pool on the television screen. It appeared that he was looking up for a way out of the pool.

Weeks went by with him thinking of that empty swimming pool and what it had meant. Was he going to drown in a swimming pool? But there was no water...what could that mean? About a month after, he received a call from a pool company that wanted him to draft designs for a swimming pool for a couple in Lansdowne. So he found that he was also getting premonitions—if he could interpret them.

Marty was quite impressed with the scientific mode the research of his skills had taken. Sara was relentless but very methodic, and he soon realized that there was much promise in using the skills. For a few months, he'd even forgotten where and how he'd acquired his abilities and how he'd used them in the jungles to survive. It was fun.

But then the shadow became darker in nature and was around much more than Marty wanted. He was still receiving images (usually positive in nature), but his personality was being affected; there was an emptiness and loneliness that was taking over. His performance at work was suffering and he no longer cared if he saw his friends or even if he worked with Sara. Nothing mattered.

Sara

Sara could not believe her luck. Not only had Marty been a good friend, but also now she'd found out that he was psychic! How cool was that? The man could name all the cards in a deck of cards, project that same deck to her, communicate at distances, tell who was on the phone—just all kinds of primo cool stuff.

But as time went by, something was changing in him. He'd never tell her about what happened specifically in Vietnam and how he came to learn the Eastern secrets of meditation and psychic ability. In fact, he was insistent that they never speak of the small country in any fashion whatsoever. That was okay with her, but she was beginning to suspect that a darker force might be behind some of his abilities. She didn't know how she knew, but this was a premonition of her own.

Regardless, she was quite vocal about his abilities, despite his trying to hide it. And most people were both surprised and interested in the things he could do. She'd begun to feel like a business manager, managing each of his demonstrations and explaining the value that each could offer in any given circumstance.

One afternoon, a Cuban friend approached her. Maria had been standing nearby as she talked about Marty to two other friends, but was not contributing to the conversation. Finally, when the two listeners left, Maria said, "Sara, I talked to my grandmother about you and Marty. She's from the old country you know. And she knows things. I was having trouble understanding her, but from what I did get, she said that the nature of Marty's abilities is evil. She told me to warn you away."

"Nonsense," replied Sara. "Marty's not evil. He's psychic."

"I didn't say Marty was evil. My grandmother said that his powers are *from* evil. And that you should be very careful that you aren't drawn into that same evil."

Sara filed her friend's advice away in the back of her mind in case there was a need to understand something that Marty did, or in case she had any more of her own premonitions. Psychic phenomenon was interesting. It seemed that the more you were around it, the more psychic you, yourself, became, even if you'd not been at all psychic before. She was now having little snippets of information come to her mind about things she had no knowledge of prior to her exposure to Marty. And it was silly stuff, like knowing to the penny how much the register was going to show at the food store before the total actually came up on the cash register. Or what the next song on the radio would be or which roads were going to be filled with traffic and therefore to be avoided. She wasn't entirely sure that the ability to do these things hadn't manifested before and she'd just not recognized them or the impact of their nature. But now she was sure that she was more tuned in than before. She had Marty to thank for that.

However, despite her best-friend status with him, and her desire to see him more in-tuned with the spiritual side of the world, she did see the truth in the advice given by her friend's grandmother. Something was changing in Marty. He was definitely more irritable and stressed over things that would've never before bothered him. If she hadn't known better, she'd swear that he had a bad case of PMS twenty-four/seven.

Working on experiments was still fun, but being with him routinely beyond that had become a chore. He required more and more attention and she'd begun to think of him as "high maintenance." Never a good thing in a friendship.

They began to spend less time together as a consequence of this change. And that very thing made things even worse. Marty became sarcastic and petty. It was during one of his strange episodes that Sara decided that not only did the experiments need to stop, but also she needed some space. She backed away.

Being young and lacking knowledge of supernatural phenomenon, Sara did not understand the dangers of pressing someone into the occult or the consequences of it, so she couldn't understand what was happening to Marty.

††††††††††††††

A couple months later, feeling much less stressed, she went out shopping and then had shopped herself out. Once back at her apartment, she closed and locked the front door, which was a habit passed onto her by her mother, who taught her that a locked door was a safe home. After unpacking her purchases, she decided that it was a good time to take a nap.

Lying down, fully clothed, on the bed, she was asleep in minutes. Suddenly though, and she didn't know exactly how long she'd been asleep, she woke with a start. The room was ice cold, though it was a warm fall afternoon. She reached over to the other side of the bed and pulled a quilt across her. Then, before she could situate the quilt just right, Sara felt pressure on her chest and across her legs. She tried to move and found she was pinned to the bed.

Her heart began to pound hard as she struggled against some invisible force laying on top of her. It felt as though someone was actually laying on top of her, pushing weight downward. She cried out. "Go away, go away!"

The pressure stayed for another three minutes or more before disappearing, but the room was still freezing cold and a wind seemed to whip around her apartment. Quickly she got up, and ran into the living room. The front door to her apartment was wide open.

The phone began to ring, making her jump. She grabbed for it.

"Hello!" she yelled into the phone, an edge to her voice that even she could hear.

"Sara, are you alright?" It was her friend Maria. "I had this feeling that I had to call you right away."

Sara started to cry as she told her of the invisible form on top her, the cold and wind, and her locked front door wide open.

"Come to my house, right away; right now, Sara!" Maria was forceful and wouldn't take no for an answer.

†††††††††††††††

At Maria's home, Sara sat at the edge of a wooden coffee table as her friend's grandmother mixed herbs in a bowl and crushed them. Maria had a photograph of Sara and her grandmother sprinkled the mixture around the photo and then lit a candle. She chanted in a language that Sara could not understand. Then she blew out the candle and spoke in soft tones to her granddaughter.

Maria turned to Sara, "She says that she's put a protective light around you and that the evil should not be able to get through now. You'll be okay."

Sara sighed. "Guess I won't be hanging out with Marty anymore..."

†††††††††††††††

Marty lay sleeping, unaware that *his* shadow person was taking over his life...or the effect it was having on those around him. He should've never allowed Sara to pressure him into a world that he did not understand.

Epilog

So, what was the invisible force that held Sara to her bed? It has been found that in some Eastern studies, a person can leave the body by astral projection and move around in the world as he or she wishes. There are those that are so strong with ability that they can even produce physical phenomena.

Can we prove that Marty came to Sara that afternoon? No. Did the Shadow person take over Marty. That, too, is unknown.

Is it possible that she had a moment of sleep paralysis? This is when there is a partial or total inability to move and occurs upon awakening or sometimes when falling asleep. This is a scientific explanation that some give for such incidents. Sara says no; she feels that Marty assaulted her that day—not in a menacing fashion, for they were still friends. But because he could—and he wanted to show her that he was still there and still thinking of her. However, the form did leave when she asked it to… And it never happened again.

Maria's grandmother advised her never to even think of it. Or him. These were dangerous thoughts that could summon other phenomena.

So have Sara and Marty learned their lessons?

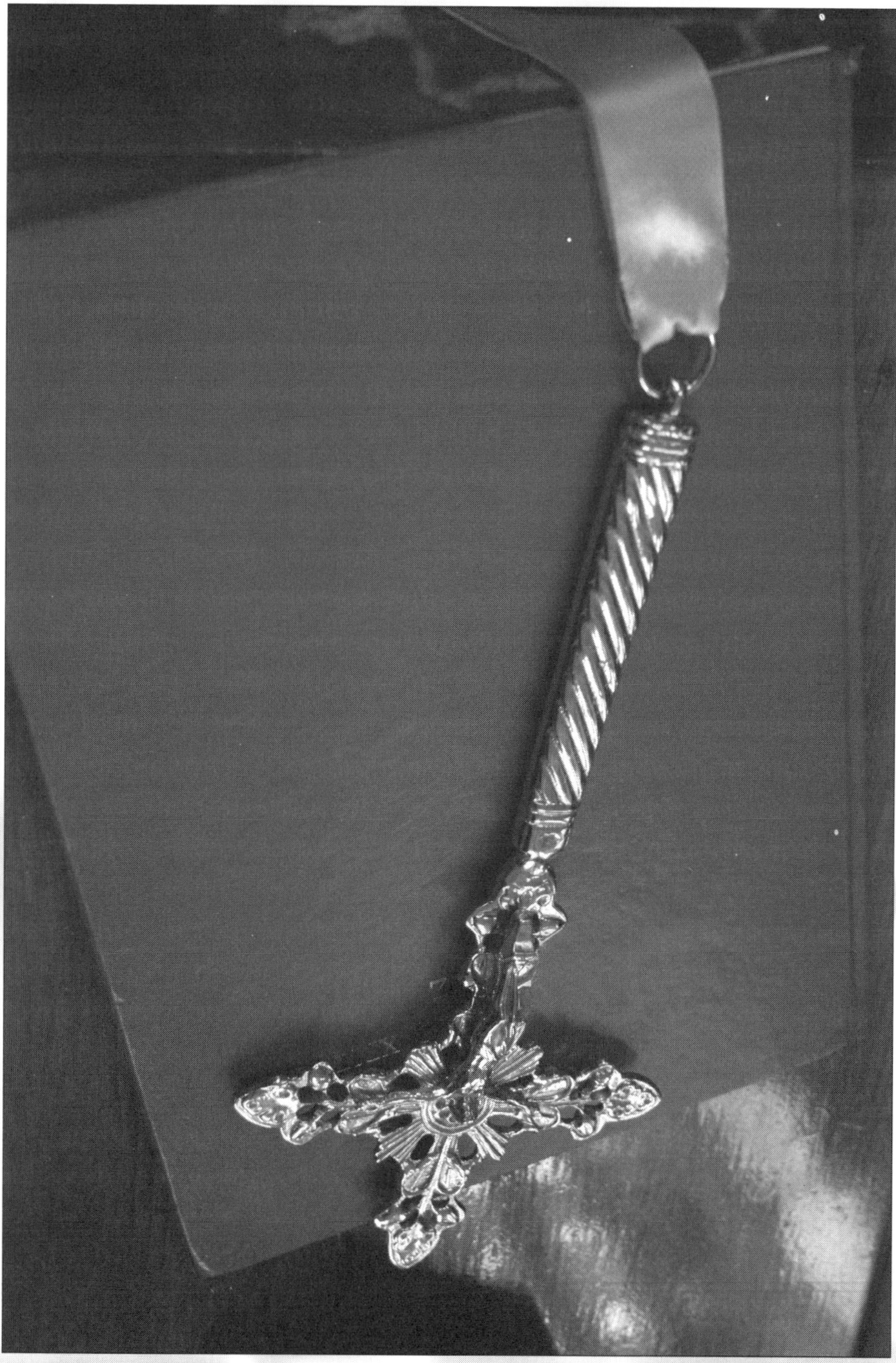

Chapter Six
It's In the Attic
Harford Road Area, Private Residence

"Whenever someone has latent abilities, they have the possibility of attracting spirits to them. These are usually spirits who have a desperate need to talk. Unfortunately, if you do not hear them, they feel they are being ignored and this can upset them."

— Ghost Quest,
New Hampshire's Paranormal Research Society

Nora hated being sick and it was even worse when that sickness lasted for an eternity—in her case nearly a week. When one was twenty and out and about in the world, kicking up heels that were in earlier times (at her parents') glued to the floor, there was no time for this foolishness. Be dammed the flu.

This was one time, however, that she was missing the doting family and the mother who brought the chicken soup and peanut butter sandwiches with just the right amount of jelly to her like clockwork whenever she was feeling ill. In her own apartment now for about three months, she had to do these mundane things for herself. And she didn't enjoy it half as much as her mother did. Oh, okay, if truth were told, she hated it. And especially when she was sick. They needed to invent some product that would take the place of a mother's cooking. *Oh, yeah, the microwave.* She cringed thinking of the three-months caked-on food on the inside top of the thing in her less than antiseptic kitchen. Who knew a baked potato would explode if you didn't puncture it first?

She'd missed three days of work already, hooked to the weekend that she'd been forced to forego because of the cold or flu or typhoid fever or malaria or whatever she had—the name didn't matter—it had put her flat on her back and out of circulation for five days with no end in sight. Further, no one she knew (her oh-so-good fair-weather friends) would come anywhere near her in fear of catching what she'd caught from someone at work who didn't stay the hell home when he was sick but came in anyway spreading his nasty germs all over the place and particularly on her. Lord! Were people stupid or what?

She could just scream. And she could if she wanted to—except that her throat hurt—and no one would hear her anyway.

She was living on the second floor of a four-apartment duplex in a small Overlea community and the owners (who lived below) had gone on vacation with the two families on the other side of the duplex—who just happened to be their grandmother or somebody (an old lady who should probably have died a while back, but didn't out of spite) and then the owner's cousin of a third cousin or something. It was surely inbreeding anyway you looked at it.

Anyway, she was alone in the house and there was no one to check on her. Except her mother who called every ten minutes it seemed, even going so far as to bribe her with a cheeseburger from McDonalds—which almost worked, but desperation of that nature had not set in just yet. She wasn't falling for that kind of tactic for another two or three days at least. Once her mother saw the state she was in—and that of her apartment—she'd never get rid of her.

Oh, and the cat. She couldn't forget the cat. It wasn't hers, but a neighborhood stray. Slinking around looking for handouts and causing general havoc with the birds that congregated at the bird-feeder on the front lawn. Damn cat. And wouldn't you know it that somehow—last Thursday night—the thing had gotten in when she'd had her hands full of groceries—he shot right through her apartment door. Now it was hiding all over the place, sneaking around with its paws all over her stuff. She hated to think where it was going to the bathroom. She hadn't smelled anything yet, but there was a reason for that. Her nose was clogged. Damn cold or flu or whatever. She'd find out about the cat pee soon enough, she was sure.

It wasn't that she didn't like cats. She did. They were better than people in most cases. It's just that she was sick and didn't have the time to search, rescue, and care for this half-grown black and white varmint with the Hitler mustache. So she'd put down a saucer of milk and cut up a leftover piece of chicken from the KFC she'd bought a week ago that had disappeared into the land of the forgotten in her refrigerator, and called it a rescue. "Catty-pie" would come out eventually and then she could boot his little behind back out to the birdbath where he could find his own breakfast. It was like all-you-can-eat day and night at the birdbath anyway for him.

She did feel a tiny bit better today, and it was a good thing, cause she'd run out of tissues the night before and was rapidly going through all the toilet paper she had blowing her nose. Her hair was unkempt, her face flushed, nose red; she was coughing and sneezing, and generally a sorry-looking thing. Nora sat down in the easy chair, the one that rocked on a base that slid back and forth, sipping ginger ale to soothe her sore throat, and watched reruns of "Quantum Leap" on the tube. (The hero should have quit after he did this show and not headed out to the stars on the next one in her opinion. He just didn't measure up to the starship, "Enterprise.")

She set down her glass of ginger ale—mostly ice now—and then watched it hop right up and onto the floor. Crash. Didn't break, just scattered ice and a bit of liquid onto the carpet. Looking at it without registering what she'd just seen, she frowned. *Damn cat,* she thought.

But the cat was nowhere around. She thought she heard him shuffling about in the kitchen behind the stove, but wasn't sure. She *was* certain, however, that she wasn't going looking for him. And if he came looking for her, he'd better have a bowl of chicken soup on his back.

Slipping out of the chair and dropping herself like a lump to the floor, she gathered the ice into the glass and dabbed at the small wet spots with already damp tissues.

"Whatever," she grumbled, as she put the glass of ice back on the end table and pulled herself up to the chair again. "I just want to die." *Ah-Choo!*

No sooner than she'd gotten herself situated in a position where she could reach the roll of toilet paper for her nose and the remote, she noticed that the glass was not on the end table. It was on the coffee table, clearly two feet in another direction.

"I’m losin' it," she mumbled. "I could've sworn…" She shrugged to herself and dismissed it.

The hours moved onward, slowly, in a dragging fashion that makes one want to cry out in agony just from boredom. Nora had taken two naps by the time dusk came, and though she was still feeling tired, the idea of going to bed or watching yet another re-run on the television was maddening. Her mother had stopped calling—this was good—because she was going away for a couple days on a much-needed vacation. Nora had reluctantly written down all the emergency numbers and taken all the notes that her mother had dictated—directions for this and that, things that any person over ten would know instinctively. She'd been too tired to protest and just did the old *Uh-huh, uh-huh* thing for a half hour. Keep the doors locked, make sure to turn the burners on the stove off so you don't burn the place down, take the medicine, drink the fluids—common sense stuff.

As the night dragged on, Nora decided that she would read for a while—that was something she hadn't done in ages. She liked to read, but never seemed to have the time. Now she had the time.

Unfortunately, though, now she didn't have the book. Looking through the bookshelf that held mostly items not remotely related to books, she tried to scavenge up a good read. There had to be something there. Trouble was, the books shelved were the ones she'd already read—Nora Roberts, Victoria Holt ... romantic intrigue was her thing. On the bottom shelf, though, mixed in with a stack of papers—*hey, there's my W-2*—was a book that someone at work had lent her to read, oh, about two years ago. It wasn't the kind of book she liked; she'd barely been able to watch the movie that followed it many years ago being a pretty scary film. But her friend said it was not only better than the movie, but was a really fun read and that it was true and all that nonsense. She pulled it out. *The Exorcist* by William Peter Blatty. It was well used to be sure and had been hanging around going from hand to hand since the 1970s. *Well,* she thought, *it's a thick one and hopefully will take me through till I'm better. May as well get started...especially since there's nothing else.*

This time, instead of the rocker, she chose the couch, sitting on it long-ways with her back against the bedroom pillows that she'd piled at one end. The coffee table was close with all needed medical paraphernalia and a warm glass of milk. She began the story of Regan's demonic possession, with a picture of Linda Blair in her mind.

It wasn't long before Nora had forgotten the world around her and had fallen deep into the land of exorcism with the Blatty book. There was the occasional sneeze and nose-blowing going on, but aside from that, she was securely held inside the strange happenings of a pretty frightening household. The book was so well written, that she could almost hear the sounds that Regan's mother was hearing. The scuttling of something overhead, the weird feel of the house...

Nora stopped reading and looked out into her living room. Had she just heard a noise? No. It was the book. Imagination hooked to the story before her. She began to read again. Some time later—well after midnight—a storm started to brew and she could hear the thunder approaching in the distance. Storms did not bother her, nor did any of the more scary things that people found frightening like the thunder and lightning. It was just nature. Oh, she'd jump alright if a loud boomer sounded when unexpected, but there was no fear involved with that. Rather it was a reaction like any other startling moment in life.

As the thunder came closer, though, she could see that Catty-Pie was not of this mind. He was scared of the thunder and was slinking his nosy little self from the kitchen to the edge of the living room, where he could keep an eye on her. Apparently, he thought that if she were okay, he would be okay. She went back to her book, ignoring him as he jumped up on the end table and curled up in a ball that appeared to just have eyes looking out of it—staring at her.

The thunder and lightning continued, and from time to time, Nora would have to look up from her book as the lights flickered in her apartment. Great. It looked like she'd have to just go to bed if all the lights went. Thank God, it was cool outside because she was sure that the little apartment would heat up like a tin can over a campfire under the right conditions.

Catty-Pie, however, was not so docile about the flickering lights and now jumped from the end table to the area just below Nora's feet.

"This little old storm can't be scaring you that much," she said to the cat when it crouched low at the next boom of thunder. "It's just sound and light. Nothing more. Well, as long as you're in here with me, that is."

She reached her hand down toward the cat, but stopped midway, frozen. The cat, too, was frozen as it peered up at the ceiling. There was scuffling coming from the attic that was located right overtop her.

At that moment, she felt a kinship with the cat. They'd both heard the sound and they'd both peered at the ceiling following an invisible trek of ...something...across the floor of the attic as it made its way from one side of the building to the other. The cat's eyes left the ceiling and centered on Nora, seeming to say, "There's something in the attic. What are you going to do about it?"

Sitting very still, the book still clutched in her hands, Nora's eyes followed the sounds above her as they moved from side to side. *Rats,* she thought at first. But then reconsidered since it would mean that these particular rats were dragging something along behind them, because that's what it sounded like. Little feet dragging something. Looking down at the book, the thought struck her that these sounds seemed like the ones that Blatty talked about in his book. And the book told of true occurrences, not just fancy.

What if there were...demons...in her attic?

The cat was now at her front door, pawing to get out—into the rainy, stormy night and where whatever was in the attic would not get him.

"Great, *now* you want to leave." Her sarcasm was thick and she didn't go to the door. "Sorry, kiddo, we're in this together."

The sounds in the attic were constant, as though whatever or whoever was up there had a pretty specific job to do; i.e., moving things from one side of the attic to another. Purpose unknown.

That night, she nor the cat got any sleep. Of course, it didn't help that the electricity finally made its threat true and went out, leaving her in the darkness with only the sounds of creatures above. Candles, though lit, just did not cut it when it came to demons in the attic. Oh, and the phone was out. Right out of a horror movie this was—or a horror book—but it wasn't fun and it wasn't entertaining. This was real stuff.

It was now she remembered things her mother had told her that she'd scoffed at. Always have lots of candles. Okay. She had two and had thought that was enough. After all, she was too old to be afraid of the dark and two candles would certainly get her from point A to point B in her apartment. What else would they be needed for? Well, wrong. Ten candles would not have been enough on this night.

And the lantern—decorative though serviceable her mother had said—was the perfect thing for electrical outages. Of course, she'd never bought lamp fluid for it, though she'd told her mother she had. That certainly would have come in handy now.

Oh and the flashlight. Now she had that, but the batteries were low and there was only a yellowish pale glow at best. She'd meant to get more batteries after that incident with her car conking out on Harford Road, but that, too, had been put on backburner.

"This is no problem," she said out loud to the cat. "I'll just get dressed and run up to the store and buy some supplies." *A-choo!* "I need more tissues anyway. More candles, tissues, batteries for the old transistor radio and the flashlight, and maybe a can of cat food. How's that sound?"

As though the cat understood what she was saying, he made his way to the front door and stood with his little nose plastered against it.

"No, you won't be going. Under other circumstances, I'd let you back out into the wilderness; but that lightning's liable to hit you and I'd never forgive myself if you got fried." The cat mewed as if to say, *Yeah, right, that's not why you want me here. You're scared of the things in the attic.*

So, despite feeling weak, foggy in the brain, and definitely sickly, Nora dressed in stretched-out sweat pants and a loose shirt, blew out the candles so that there'd be no accidental burning down of the place (*thank you very much Mother*, she thought) grabbed her jacket, and with umbrella in hand, made her way to the 7-11. She scooted out the door, pushing the cat back inside as she moved out into the hallway. Unfortunately—or fortunately, whichever way you chose to view it—the attic was not reachable from inside Nora's apartment. There was a trap door that came down out of the hallway ceiling just outside her front door. Once there on the landing, she stared up at the trap door contraption leading up to the attic—she could see glimpses of it from the lightning outside that lit up the stairwell through the glass at the bottom of the downstairs door to the outside.

The attic sounds were faint from this location, merely a soft scuffling. *Easily a rat*, she thought, but then dismissed it. Inside the apartment, *it* had sounded like a party. There was something up there alright and it was bigger than a rat. But it couldn't be a demon, she thought, jumping as another thunderbolt seemed to rock her to the bone. Demons didn't party. It was rats. Yes, that's what it was—had to be. No, wait. Squirrels. They were industrious creatures and she knew they were about because she'd seen Catty-Pie bring down one or two. A gross sight to be sure.

The lightning that followed brought her from her thoughts and she raced down the stairs in the dark—not difficult since she'd done that many times when the hall light had been blown. ...And wasn't that interesting? How often that hall light was blown...

"Stop it!" she said out loud to herself. "No wonder I'm freaked out. I'm imagining all kinds of things." She pushed the thought of the hall light from her mind and stepped out into the thunderous storm.

Her car started without issue, something she'd been worried about—because if indeed there were demons in the attic and they'd knocked out the lights, and were partying hardy, they'd not feel real kindly about her leaving the premises. She'd seen all the movies and knew the drill. If the situation were a real monster situation, well then her car wouldn't start.

But it did, so she was safe.

At the 7-11, she was unable to get candles or lamp oil, but she got her tissues, two cans of cat food, and enough batteries for the radio and flashlight. The flashlight would have to do, along with the two candles she had. And out in the real world, she felt that what she had would be plenty enough.

She smiled at the cashier who had an unearthly glow about him. "I see you have your lights," she said, trying to be friendly, but more wanting to hear another's voice.

"Yeah," he replied in a tone that said *Duh*.

Nora wasn't offended though. There were few people out and about on this terrible night and even this small encounter with an odd individual was inviting. "Mine are out," she said, "thus the batteries."

The cashier merely nodded and pushed the bag of items toward her. "Have a nice night," he said.

She looked up into his eyes and they seemed to take on the glow from the fluorescents shining in from the street as they bounced off the rain. "If you can," he added.

Nora gulped. She certainly hadn't needed that little vernacular of terror. Suddenly she felt like she was in a Frankenstein movie. She sighed hard and then made her way back out into the rain and to her waiting apartment.

Once outside the duplex, however, she sat in her car, just looking up at her second-floor apartment window. Had she seen movement through the pounding rain? The water slid down her windshield in torrents, providing a movement all its own, but still, just beyond the water, just beyond the night, she thought she saw the curtain move at the front window. This was not good. But it had to be her imagination again, or that Catty-Pie. It could be him, she thought, a small hope filtering through a throbbing fear sensation that was attempting to break through. That's what it was...*who* it was...it was the Catty-Pie.

Pulling her hood close about her, opening the car door, and flipping the inflate switch to her umbrella popping it open wide, she made her way up the front porch of the house. Struggling with her key, she finally inserted it into the keyhole, but to her surprise the door swung open by itself.

So there she stood, umbrella blowing in the wind with streams of water flowing over its edges to the cement beneath her, her hand outstretched with the key towards the door, and her body frozen in time. She'd locked the door behind her. She clearly remembered doing so. This was not good.

But something even more strange was afoot. The hall light was on just beyond the now-open door and she could see that the trap door at the top of the stairs was open, as though someone had pulled it down and ventured into its dark recesses of the attic. She stepped back from the door and walked backwards down the three cement steps till she was on flat ground. There was *someone* in the house.

Looking up at her apartment window through the rain, she remembered the movement she'd seen. The rooms throughout the house were still dark indicating that the electricity was still out. She'd left on the living room lamp so she'd know when the power was back. Glancing back around her at the other homes in the neighborhood, she saw that they, too, were dark. Of course, it was midnight by now and most people would be sleeping. Still, there was always those chosen few night dwellers who stayed up to watch late-night television or did other things that required their night attention.

But not tonight. The neighborhood was dark. The house before her holding her second-floor apartment was dark. The only light visible was the one on in the hallway leading up to the trap door.

It was time to call the police.

Nora quickly ran back to her car and hopped inside, pulling her purse open for her cell phone. "This cannot be happening," she said to no one. "I *did not* leave my phone on the end table. I *did not* do that."

But she had. *Now what?* she thought. *I'm not doing something stupid like going in there and checking on things myself. That's what the stupid girl always does. And then she ends up dead or a living-dead zombie or is eaten by an alien.*

"Back to the 7-11," she said out loud, speedily backing out of the driveway. "I'll call the police from there. Momma didn't raise no dummy." Then she whispered as she made her way through the deserted streets, "Hang in there Catty-Pie..."

At the 7-11, she was in luck, for a Parkville patrol car was sitting on the lot and the officer was standing at the checkout inside.

She hurried in. "Excuse me, Officer? I was just here to buy a few things and then when I went back to my apartment, the door was open when I'd locked it and the trap door to the attic was down. I think someone's in there. Someone broke in while I was out!"

"Calm down, Miss," he said, but she could see that the adrenalin in him was beginning to pump. "What's your address? I'll go check it for you."

Nora quickly answered his questions and then both she and the officer headed back to her apartment. On the way, they picked up three more patrol cars and they all arrived at her place in a line and a blaze of lights, blinding red flashes reflecting on the falling rain. The officers were out of their cars in an instant and hastened carefully up to her front door. Two slipped around each side of the house to make sure the rear was secure.

But Nora stood stock still, her umbrella hanging on the ground at her side and filling with rain. She watched the officers at her front door. It was securely closed and apparently locked. There was no light shining through the top glass frames of the door. The house was dark.

She ran up the steps behind the officers. "That door was open and unlocked when I left here a few minutes ago! And the hall light was on!"

"The lights in the whole neighborhood are off, Miss. There's no way a light could have been on in there. Maybe flashlights?"

That put the officers on further alert. They immediately dismissed Nora's hall light explanation and provided their own intuitive answer to a light source in a community without power.

"But the door...." began Nora. "It was locked and then it was opened and now it's locked again."

The officers still ignored her. "Key, Miss? Do you have the key?" one asked.

She handed it over to him in resignation. Could they be right? Had she imagined seeing the door open and the light on? She was after all quite sick. Nora stood back as the officers unlocked the door and ventured into the tight hallway. Over their shoulders, she could see from their flashlights that the trapdoor was closed. They made their way up the stairs and now stood in front of her apartment door.

"This your apartment?"

Nora nodded and scrunched up the stairs among the officers. She pointed to the appropriate key on her ring and he unlocked the door. "Back down stairs, Miss," one officer said and ushered her away from the apartment door and out of harm's way.

They opened the door. It was then that the lights for the entire community came back on—streetlights, porch lights, lights inside homes. The light left on inside Nora's apartment gave glow to a messy, sick home. Peeking around from the couch was Catty-Pie, looking like he'd seen a ghost as he peered up at the men. In an instant, he darted for the door, ran out, and hit the steps practically flying. Nora caught him on the way down.

"Calm down, Catty-Pie; we're okay now." She held tight to the cat as the officers went through her entire apartment and then beckoned her up and inside.

"There's no one here, Miss," said the officer from the 7-11. "You must've imagined that door being open and the light. And the trap door."

Nora stood still trying to listen to note whether she could hear the noises from the attic, but all was quiet now. She looked up at the ceiling.

"Do you want us to check upstairs?" the officer inquired.

She nodded and the cat squirmed in her arms. This was a good thing. She'd know once and for all...

So out into the hallway, they went—though most had to stand on the stairs or inside her doorway to fit. They pulled down the trap door stairway and the officer went upstairs into the attic. Nora held her breath.

In a moment, the officer called down. "There's nothing up here at all. Very clean. Nothing here. Miss, would you like to see?"

No, thought Nora, *not for all the tea in China.* "Yes," she said, and handed the cat to another officer, who wrinkled his nose, put the cat into the apartment, and closed the door so it wouldn't escape.

Gulping (and sniffling), Nora climbed the few steps up to the attic and held out the flashlight that another of the officers had given her. She flashed the light around and saw nothing but the officer. There was nothing but a few boxes at the edges of one side overtop her portion of the house and the floor was dust-covered. The only disturbance to that dust was the footprints of the police officer. Nothing was out of place, and nothing gave any indication that anything was—or had ever been—there in that dark place. Much less a rodent party.

So it was that the officers left her, trying to tell her that storms often caused effects that appeared differently than under normal circumstances. They spoke of imaginations running wild when thunder was loud and lightning fierce. She felt stupid.

Once they'd left and she was snugly back in her own space, she fed the cat, and took her next round of cold remedy. This was baloney, she thought, slamming the cupboard doors. She'd heard something in the attic and so had the cat. The door had been locked and then it wasn't. The light was off; then it was on; then it was off again when the power was out. The trap door had been open. She was not crazy and certainly not the type to make up stories for attention. (She'd seen the look on one of the officer's faces. He pitied her. Damn them anyway.)

There was no sleeping till the Benedryl kicked in, so she sat again with the book in her lap and the cat purring next to her. Looks like she had a cat now. Then suddenly, she heard something. The cat heard it too, and looked up at the ceiling.

Within seconds, the ceiling overhead sounded as though it would give way as the creatures moved from side to side again. Only this time, she could swear they were rolling bowling balls across the floor. With shaking hands, she picked up her newly battery-loaded flashlight, slipped on her slippers, and went into the hallway outside her apartment door. The trap door steps were down again. The hall light was on and she could see that the door downstairs to the outside was still dead-bolted from inside.

She had to know. The bowling sounds became louder as she moved cautiously up step by step to the open attic space. The opening was a dark hole into a black nothingness that seemed to urge her forward towards some nightmare from which she would never awake. Catty-Pie began to mew behind her, still inside the door to her apartment, as if to implore her not to go further.

At the top step, all the sounds ceased. There was no scuffling, no bowling balls rolling from side to side. Silence reached out to her and only the distant roll of thunder from a storm now passing could be heard. That...and her heartbeat.

Nora shined the light into the black space and again saw only an empty attic and no disturbance in the dust on the floor beyond that of the police officer. Something, though, made her shine the light upward…and she screamed out.

There, hanging on a nail overtop the door was a rosary, the one her mother had given her. The rosary was hanging upside down. She grabbed it and half fell back down the stairs. Inside her apartment, she locked the door and held the rosary close to her chest—she'd seen it last when it was with her grandmother, in her casket at her funeral, her last gift to someone she loved.

Whatever was in the attic was not of this world. It had stolen the rosary from her grandmother and it was there now to steal something from her.

††††††††††††††

When the owner of the duplex and his relations returned home from their trip, they found an empty second-floor apartment.

Nora had seen all the movies and knew all the worst-case scenarios. She would not be staying in a haunted house or a place that had a demon resident. She would not allow a creature from the other side to chide her with its antics. Instead, she'd moved all her belongings back to her mother's house. That was one place she—and her cat, Catty-Pie—could be safe. And sick—in peace.

Epilog

I'm afraid that our entertainment these days—and I'm as much to blame as anyone for this—has desensitized us to the truth sitting right outside factual realities. We watch devils and demons on the tube and the big screen and cower beneath our covers and jackets. We read horror novels—really good ones! We buy into the world of what we call fantasy. And there's no harm in that.

The harm comes when we hide behind those things and don't recognize that there is, indeed, a real side to devils and demonology; and that there are more and more cases of such things coming to light every day.

Katie Boyd, a demonologist for over nineteen years, says it best:

> *"We have always been taught one basic truth: where there is good, there is bad; for every good day you have, inevitably, there will be a bad day. It is called polarity, however, most of us aren't cognizant of this phenomena spiritually. Most of us can recognize evil when we see it, whether human or otherwise; it is built into our DNA, this sensitivity to danger. It's our mechanism for survival, hence why when we sense someone is a 'danger,' for instance, and then cross the street when they come in our path. Demonic entities and homes that are haunted trigger this same mechanics; it is a feeling of fear, and a driving need to hide or leave."*

And, one thing to remember is something that she has chillingly put into words in this way:

> *What you can see in this world can hurt you, but what you can't can kill you. Be prepared.*

My advice? Don't mess around with this stuff. Call in the professionals! And keep your mom's address close by!

Chapter Seven

Witchy Woman

Parkville / Loch Raven Areas

"Ever mind the Rule of Three, three times what thou givest returns to thee, this lesson well, thou must learn, thee only gets what thou dost earn."

— The Threefold Law of Wiccan

Rayna was in love. There was no doubt. No thinking about the pros and cons of dating a police detective in Baltimore County. No considering the lifestyles and habits of the men who so valiantly solved the worst crimes in the region.

It had been a blind date, which in the past had not always been a fruitful endeavor for Rayna. Oh yes, she'd had her *doozies* in days past involving men who were so far off the geek meter or self-indulgent scale, or just so creepy that it was sad, when it had come to her match-making friends and their blind fantasies of her love life. But this time, her friend, Gina, had hit a bull's eye. She'd found the perfect man.

Rayna frowned. Perfect was always a scary prospect, since she'd witnessed first hand that no man was perfect. Far from it in her experience. She'd fallen down that staircase one too many times. Whether it was the control freak that she'd just dumped or the two-faced liar who'd dumped *her* the time before that, all were there in multitudes at her door. She had a sign on her forehead apparently: *Jerks and losers welcome here.*

Ah, but this one... Brad was different. She'd been dating him for over a month now exclusively. He was a gentleman, so smart and charismatic, and he simply adored her. She could tell by the way he had held her hand across the table at the Beloc Diner that first night and how he stared into her eyes later as they danced the night away at the Sheraton in Towson. The evening had been so much fun. They'd met at the Beloc for coffee that lasted well through dinner and then window-shopped at Towsontown where he'd bought her the cutest little skunk stuffed animal. Then they'd walked across the bridge over the boulevard and into the Sheraton for dancing at the lounge there. It had been some time since anyone had taken her on a real date. And this one would go down in infamy as one of the best.

Gina and her new boyfriend had joined them at the club for dancing, and Rayna and her friend had giggled in the ladies room over their good fortune. Gina's cop boyfriend had suggested the blind date for his roommate after meeting Rayna the prior week. It was a perfect set up. Best friends dating best friends. Life was sweet.

But, of course, as relationships developed in Rayna's life, so did the downhill tumble of emotional suicide. Rayna got too close too quick and Brad pulled away as though he'd been stung by a thousand bees. It was no matter to him that he'd told Rayna that he loved her. That he'd shared her bed. That he'd met her family. That he'd even mentioned marriage in passing. The signals he gave off were those inviting closeness and a formal relationship. Rayna responded in kind.

Unfortunately (for Rayna), Brad was a player and a womanizer. During the day, he was an upstanding, honest, and dedicated police detective who could be trusted with anyone's life. But come nighttime, that honesty turned to games and moral degradation for any woman believing his brown-eyed lies. And Rayna had been such a believer—hook, line, and sinker.

"I'm really sorry I set you up with him, Rayna. I didn't know he was such a jerk." Gina was indeed horrified that she'd been so wrong in thinking that Brad was the perfect match for her friend. "He seemed so nice and sincere…"

Rayna merely shrugged, misery etched on her face. "He hasn't called in two weeks, Gina. He's not returned one of my calls."

"You've got to stop calling him, Ray," offered Gina. "He's bad news and you just have to move on."

"I can't," she said, a tear falling down her face. "I love him."

Gina just shook her head. "Bad news, girl. This was a mistake." Gina paused as if trying to decide whether to tell her something or keep it to herself.

"What?" asked Rayna. "I know you. And you know something. Tell."

"I don't know if I should," hedged Gina. "You won't like it and it will probably make things worse than they are."

"Well you can't not tell me now." Rayna was bracing herself by holding on to the edge of Gina's kitchen table. "Hit me."

"Okay…I guess…" Still Gina stopped, but when she saw that Rayna was not going to let her off, she continued. "I was at Jonathan's apartment and Brad was home, too."

Rayna nodded, gulping.

"He wasn't alone. He had another girl with him. And they were a couple. Like you and he were a couple."

Rayna turned away, her stomach churning and tears flowing down her face. "How could he do that to me?"

"It's what jerks do. Come on Ray, he's not worth it. There's someone out there for you. I just know it."

Rayna nodded again and made her excuses to leave. She needed to suffer in peace.

Famous Last Words

Days turned into nights, nights into weeks, weeks into months. Rayna suffered. Her job performance was falling because she could not focus on the tasks at hand. Her studies at Dundalk Community College were failing—she missed classes so often due to the depression she'd sunken into. She didn't go out to have fun, she'd lost way too much weight, and didn't really care if she lived. All she could think of was Brad.

The next semester at the college was upon her. Though she'd barely passed her classes in the prior one, she decided that she'd take a class in stress management. That at least might help her move beyond her continual self-pity and pining for something that was never going to happen. Brad would not be coming back.

She'd tried calling him, leaving messages on his answering machine about them just being friends. (Even that would be better than not having him at all.) She'd driven by his apartment hoping to catch a glimpse of him in the parking lot. She frequented his nearby grocery store and went to the places he hung out. Nothing had helped. So she suffered alone.

One evening, during a break in her stress management class, she overheard another student talking about a love spell that could be put on a guy to make him more accessible in the relationship department. She struck up a conversation with the woman.

Apparently this woman knew a woman, who knew a woman—sounded shady to Rayna—who was a witch. And this witch would, for a fee, put a love spell on someone. It was interesting and Rayna casually took the phone number when it was offered. She'd never talked to a witch before. Her mind was filled with images of broomsticks and cranky old ladies around a cauldron. She wasn't sure she'd call, but she might. Desperation was a funny thing.

The class that night cinched it though. A piece of the curriculum dealt with how people used religion as a calming factor in their lives—a way to connect to something bigger than themselves. The Wiccan religion came up and Rayna learned about intention and how such intention could be used in various spells—if done carefully and correctly. This was something that some people did with success apparently. The teacher warned students "not to try this at home." It was a risky business and could have dire outcomes. This was nothing to be trifled with.

So the next day, Rayna called the scribbled number that she'd taken from her classmate to make an appointment with the witch. She'd decided that letting Brad go was not something she was willing to do. He loved her. She knew he did. This was just his way of handling the fear of commitment to her. A love spell was just what the doctor ordered. Brad needed to be brought around to her way of thinking.

But things weren't quite that easy. It seemed that in order to secure a private appointment with the Priestess Genene, one had to take a class with her first. The class consisted of four consecutive Tuesday nights, two hours each night, and delved into the world of Wiccan, so that students would not only understand the religion but the connection that each individual had with the earth and the universe, regardless of their views of any other religion. She had expected a more traditional-looking witch and was surprised to see that Genene was much like her. She didn't wear black or a witch's hat, but rather a mauve pantsuit, hair swept up in a ponytail, and Mary Kay makeup that first night of class.

Truth be told, the class was fun and enlightening. Rayna had dragged Gina along with her and both women came away with knowledge and understanding of a world that had previously eluded them. This mini-course had value.

Once completed, Rayna then set up her appointment with the Priestess for a spell consultation. Rayna had no idea that the whole love spell thing was so complicated. The witch was careful about such things and talked with her at length about the feasibility of such a spell and the repercussions of it.

"You must be absolutely sure that this is something that you want," said Genene in her private talk with Rayna. "It's not something that can be undone with any ease, if at all. I can't say that I really recommend it. Go home and think a while. Then let me know."

Rayna was nonplussed at being sent away, but dutifully left the kind witch and spent the following weekend thinking of all the pros and cons about the love spell. The fact was, she could not think of a single con. She had gotten a bit miffed at Gina though when she suggested that maybe a love secured in this way might not be a true love. How silly was that? Brad cared for her. She knew it and she wasn't some silly woman following a schoolgirl crush. Yes, there were issues, to be sure. Brad was afraid of commitment to one woman. That was a major hurdle. But she knew that she was the one woman who could—and would—change that.

Her decision was made.

The following Friday night, after Wiccan class, Rayna met with Genene to talk about the spell.

Genene was, again, very cautioning with Rayna. "You must be sure."

"I am. I swear I am sure and this is the right thing."

"Very well, then. I must say that you may not hold me responsible for this spell. The outcome is your own doing. You will perform the spell yourself and with your own specific intention. I will instruct you how."

This surprised Rayna. She'd thought that Genene would be performing the spell and that she would just be sitting there receiving the bounty. But, no, Genene spent the better part of the next hour telling her what she needed to buy in way of supplies, explaining the timing of the moon's cycles, giving her the incantation to use, and telling her how to prepare for the spell.

"It's all about intention," she told Genene. "Your intention. Your belief. Your will." Then she looked deeply into Rayna's eyes and said, "You must be careful what you wish for, my friend."

The Spell

That weekend, Rayna made her way around town to varied stores for the supplies she would need to conduct the spell on the next full moon—which was only three days away. Gina had wanted to come along, but Genene was very specific with the instruction that her entire spell—the preparation for, and the spell itself—be totally secretive. No one must know any part of it or the love would not come; the spell would be void.

She bought each item she needed from a different store. The roses came from the cold storage flower refrigerator at the Giant Food Store at Loch Raven and Taylor. The jeweled box and meditation music came from the Hallmark store in Towsontown Shopping Center. There was already a photo of her and Brad, taken at the Loch Raven Dam, that would go inside the box. She also already had incense—ginger for success and empowerment and lavender for love, though she hadn't known what each had meant prior to Genene telling her. The lavender soap and bath beads came from Bath and Body Works in White Marsh Mall and she'd picked up a red candle for sexuality at the Target on Putty Hill. She was set.

††††††††††††††††

Three days later as the full moon came into view, she began the ritual to bring Brad's love back to her. First, she bathed in a warm tub of water filled with lavender bath beads and using the lavender bath soap to cleanse away her prior skin. Rose pedals graced the top of the water and floated around her body as she lounged, thinking loving thoughts of her and Brad. The idea was to visualize what she wanted to happen, how she wanted her love with him to be. She was to meditate to the soft music, knowing that what she wanted would be delivered to her.

When her bath was done, she put on the prettiest teddy she had in her closet—white with small rosebuds at the breast line. At the coffee table in her living room, now placed in front of the patio door window in full sight of the moon, she lit the red candle.

"For warmth and love and desire bright, I light this candle in the night," she whispered.

The incense came next and, as she lit the two stems, a soft scent of herbal wonder floated through the air. She whispered as she lit the lavender fragrance...

"With this scent I send to you, my love and promise to be true."

Then, with the ginger incense stick...

"I only ask your love come back to me—times one, times two, and now times three."

Next to the candle and incense lay the photo of the two of them, the jewel box, and a handful of rose pedals. She lifted the lid to the box and placed the rose pedals inside as a bed for the photograph she placed atop them and then closed the lid to the box. More rose pedals were spread around the box.

"And now my spell of love is done. I wait with desire for my special one. He now is far, but soon so near; his love for me will not disappear. So Mote It Be."

She then sat there in front of the moon and meditated about their lives intertwined until 3 a.m. in the morning as instructed by Genene. With that finally completed, Rayna blew out the candle, but left the small alter in front of the window. She went to bed knowing that the next day would be a momentous one for her. Brad would be back.

†††††††††††††††

Before she knew it, the birds outside her window were chirping their morning song, forcing Rayna to open her pretty blue eyes. It was time to get up and enjoy the first day of the rest of her life. For that's how she felt. She just knew the spell she'd cast had worked and that this day would be *the* day.

Going about her business this fine-weathered weekend, she kept her cell phone with her on loud ring the whole time. She had her hair done. She had her nails done. She went to the gym. And, finally, she came home, showered, and waited by her home telephone with her cell phone sitting right next to it. She practiced how she would take the call, what she would say to him, how she would welcome him back. Should she scold him for his mistakes? Probably not. No sense testing the spell too much at this early date. But she would be cool and calm, ready for the challenge that lay ahead.

At midnight, after she'd watched every stinking television show she could to keep awake, she realized that this must be a work day for Brad and that he probably would not be able to call her that evening. There was definitely a reason for the call not coming. He was certainly tied up with an important case. She couldn't, after all, expect him to drop his detective responsibilities. Men lived for their jobs. Tomorrow was another day.

Tomorrow came and went. Rayna told herself that there were certainly mitigating circumstances for him not responding to the spell. Still, she was worried and called Genene.

"Give it a little time," counseled Genene. "It takes time for these things. Sometimes they work right away; sometimes it takes a bit longer. But don't be discouraged. Just go about your life. It will happen. He will be back."

After a month of waiting and pining, however, Rayna was not certain. She'd cried her way through the time waiting and, though, Genene had advised her not to contact him, she'd called him—only a couple times though. He'd never taken her calls. His voice mail always came on at his home and on his cell; and the secretary at his office only took messages.

Another month passed. Now she was angry—at him, at herself, at Genene, at Gina for introducing them, at the world. She spent much of her time alone now, because no one wanted to be with her. The whining and complaining and crying turned people away after a while. She knew what she was doing to her life, but she couldn't help it. She loved Brad and she knew that all she needed was one little chance to prove to him that they could be happy together.

One of Rayna's interests was horseback riding and she routinely went to a stable in Hunt Valley to ride, maybe once or twice a month. With no friends to spend time with, and Brad not cooperating, she began to spend more and more time at the stables, sending all her love and affection to the horse she rode and had labeled as her own. It seemed that those riding jaunts were the only solace for her weary mind. She began to stop by the stables, if not to ride, then to groom the horse, everyday after work and would spend all of Saturday and Sunday there. She grew away from the world.

She had completed nearly three months of waiting for the spell to work and for Brad to finally realize that he belonged with her when she noticed that a man was watching her as she worked with the horse. At first, she dismissed him, but then began to notice that he was there most of the times when she was riding. She began to look for him and was aware when he wasn't about.

This was strange behavior for a woman who was spoken for, she thought. However, she didn't feel too badly sneaking a peek at him to see what he was up to under the circumstances. Very cute, he was. A full head of blondish-brownish hair, a mustache that curled around his mouth, not too tall (but not too short either), well dressed in fashionable stable attire—i.e. decent jeans and flannel shirt; cute. And a nice smile.

Yikes! He was smiling at her!

Pushing back her guilt, she smiled back at him and led the horse in the opposite direction, going for her ride like always. When she returned to the stables, he was still there, but busy working with one of the other horses, trying to dislodge something from its hoof. He looked up as she brought her own horse into the stable.

"Hi," he said pleasantly. "I'm Josh."

"Rayna," she answered.

Rayna forgot Brad.

All's Well That Ends Well—Sorta Kinda

Rayna had been dating Josh for a month when she finally had time to have lunch with Gina. "I'm sorry I've been so distant. That Brad thing really had me, but I'm okay now. In fact, I'm dating someone new."

"Well, I'm certainly glad to hear that. I'm sorry I've been distant, too. I just didn't know how to help you. I mean, you were obsessed. It was like a spell was put on *you* instead of him!"

They spent the afternoon catching up on news and chattering about Josh and how much better he was than Brad. Josh, an engineer with steady daytime hours, was a joy. Not only was he visually appealing to Rayna, but he was respecting, sensible, exciting—just every positive adjective she could think of.

They'd been lovers for about a week, and this time, rather than playing at longevity, he'd come right out and asked her to date him exclusively and that he would do the same for her. Then he'd given her a ring. It was an opal—not a diamond—but that was okay. It was symbolic. Rayna was very happy. Gina had been right. There'd been someone else out there for her. And in fact, had she not been through the Brad thing, she wouldn't have spent all that time at the stables and she'd never had met Josh. Or at least, she'd never have known how wonderful he was.

This was a classic case of understanding that everything happened for a reason.

†††††††††††††††

It was a Sunday night on a night of the full moon when the first phone call came—rather Monday morning early. Something had woken Rayna up to watch the clock click over to 3 a.m. She yawned and stretched noting that she had three more hours to sleep before getting up for work. It was than that her home phone burst forth with a loud ring tone she'd not heard before, startling the cobwebs from her sleepy mind.

"What the hell?" she said out loud, wondering not only who would be calling her at this time, but also what that strange ring tone was all about. "Has to be an emergency," she whispered, thinking of her parents immediately.

"Hello?" she said into the receiver, nearly dropping it as she reached for it.

"Rayna? Rayna, honey?" the voice said.

Rayna frowned. The voice was familiar, but not. There was a slur to the words and a cracking of a male voice. "Yes?" she said tentatively. "Who is this?"

"It's me, Brad," he said. "I'm so sorry…"

Rayna was shocked, but further, there was a knot in her stomach that was forcing its way up to her throat. This was Brad on the other end of the phone line at 3 a.m. in the morning sounding very much inebriated. It had been four months and now it was three in the morning. "It's late," she said, trying to keep the annoyance from her voice. Two months ago, she would have been elated even at this inconsiderate time of the morning. But now, with Josh filling her every need, she'd seen the folly of her interest in the self-indulgent Brad. And now here he was. "What do you want?"

"I want to make everything up to you; I want to see you, hold you; I can't live without you…"

He sounded so drunk. *Great,* she thought, *the only time he calls is when he's too drunk to think.* And too late for her to appreciate the limited gesture.

"Go sleep it off," she snapped. "I have to work in the morning. Good night, Brad."

"No, no, don't go!" she could hear him say as she hung up the phone.

The phone rang again. She ignored it and let it go to the answering machine. It was him, of course, leaving a mushy, drunk message. She turned off the ringer to all the phones and went back to bed, noting that now she only had about two hours before she had to get up.

The phone rang again at 4 a.m.

"Now that's just not possible," she said out loud, throwing a pillow to the wall and picking up the telephone. She didn't answer, but turned the contraption over in her hands to see if the ringer was shut off. It was on.

"I shut that off. I know I shut it off."

Still it rang, and this time did not go to the answering machine. Rayna got up and went out into the living room to look at the machine. It was off just as it should be. But the phones should've been off too and then there was that weird ring again. She unplugged the phones from the wall.

At 5 a.m., her cell phone rang and, asleep again, she just reached for it out of habit and said, "Hello?"

"Rayna?" said the slurred voice, "It's Brad; don't hang up." He was crying now and the voice brought her awake in a panic.

"What do you want, Brad; what is wrong?"

"I was wrong to leave you, take me back. I love you. Marry me. We belong together forever."

He was obnoxious and so drunk that she could barely understand the words. "Brad, I can't talk with you like this. Call me when you've slept it off. We can talk, but I'm not taking you back."

"But I love you and you love me and I'm ready to commit!" He stumbled over the word commit.

Remembering clearly that it was never fruitful arguing with a drunk, she merely said, "Yeah, yeah, call me tomorrow—at a more respectable hour. I have to go now. Go to bed, Brad." And she hung up before he could stammer out another protest.

††††††††††††††††

When the alarm went off at 6 a.m, Rayna was dragging. She managed to get through the day, though, and was oddly relieved that Brad had not called her back. *Still hung over,* she thought. But hung over or not, she'd felt nothing during the encounter with him. She was over him and now clearly saw the bullet she'd dodged. He was a womanizer…and a drunk—and about a million other negative things. There was no way he could outshine—or even hold a glimmer—to the wonderful man Josh was.

The anger had set in as well, for she'd made a complete fool of herself over him. The eyes of love had hidden from her that he was a control freak, a liar, a cheat, and had no business in a relationship with any self-respecting woman. What had she been thinking? She'd actually thought she could change him! And she knew that one person couldn't change another. She'd seen all the *Oprah* shows about it and read all the relationship books. It was as though she'd been wearing blinders.

Then she remembered the physiology behind feelings of love. Nature took care to adorn lovers with those rose-colored glasses to promote procreation. It was a fact. And she'd been held in the midst of that passion for months. This gave her pause, because she was in a similar state with Josh at this very moment. Rayna made note to talk with Gina about it just in case colored lenses were blinding her yet again.

The week went by without issue and Rayna settled back into her life with Josh. She was deliriously happy and further pleased that all her friends assured her that Josh was indeed a catch and not like Brad in any way. She was not blind to faults this time.

But though it would be nice to say that all ended well, it didn't happen that way. The very next Monday morning at 3 a.m., her phone rang that crazy ring again. Rayna awoke with a start and recognized the ring immediately. This was truly bizarre—she'd have to have another look at the phone manual to see why that ring kept occurring. She didn't want to answer it, but she was curious.

"Hello?" she said and stopped, not making a sound. All she could hear was whimpering on the other side of the phone line.

Then finally, "I miss you, Ray…come back. Don't make me suffer like this. I was wrong; I'm sorry."

Drunk again, thought Rayna. *Why is this guy calling me in the middle of the night?*

It was then that the light bulb came on in her mind. *It couldn't be the love spell. The spell didn't work.* She pushed it from her mind.

During the week, she scoured the telephone manual that came with her phone and found that the ring tone she'd heard was not part of the phone's setup. *Now how can that be?* she wondered. The spell. *No.* It hadn't worked.

That next Sunday night after Josh had left for the evening, she went around to each phone in her home and unplugged it from the wall and she turned off her cell phone. *No sense taking chances,* she thought. *I don't want to ever hear from him again. Maybe some of his own game is in order here. I just won't answer his calls.*

She slept all night that night, but there was a restlessness to her sleep. And at 3 a.m., she opened her eyes and looked at the clock. *Man,* she thought, *this is weird.* But she was quickly able to go back to sleep. The next day when she turned on her cell, there were seventeen messages from Brad—each more pathetic than the last, begging her to come back, to answer his calls, to forgive him.

Again, her week went by smoothly. She saw Josh every evening after work and retired at about ten each night. Then Sunday night came. So paranoid she was about the Brad calls, she once more unplugged her phones and turned off the cell. At three in the morning, she awoke and glanced at the clock. *This is ridiculous,* she thought. *It can't be that darn spell. Wouldn't it just be my luck, though?*

Seconds after thinking how ridiculous the entire telephone situation was, she heard a loud pounding on her door. "Rayna!" Brad called out from the other side and he must have fallen, because she heard a crash and then his voice was at floor level. "Rayna," he cried. "Please let me in!"

His voice was loud and drunk and he kept calling her name sounding like a sick child. "Go home, Brad! You're drunk and you'll wake up my neighbors!" She wasn't about to open the door to him.

"No, don't send me away my love, my Rayna, my life! I can't live without you!"

Just then she heard a door open across the hall. "Give it a rest, pal! It's three in the morning. Get out or I'll call the police!"

She could hear him scuffle away from her door and toward her neighbor's apartment. *Oh no!*

"I *am* the police, *pal*," he slurred to the neighbor. "So you just go inside and leave me be."

He turned back now to Rayna's door apparently because with her eye to the peephole she was startled at the loud pounding that he resumed. "Let me in Rayna! I mean it, let me in!"

In the distance, she could hear the police sirens coming. Brad must have heard them too, because he stumbled down the hall and out of eye and earshot. The building was quiet again.

...until the next weekend when it happened again. And the week after.

It wasn't long before the apartment complex wanted her out—there was too much drama for the other tenants. And now, despite her best efforts of concealing it, Josh had found out that Brad was stalking her. He wanted her to press charges, but didn't he know that you never press charges against a cop? Because then you would have *all* of them after you for every little minor thing!

Before another Sunday night could go by, Rayna went to see Genene to tell her what had been happening.

"I was afraid of something like this. There are some loves that one just doesn't chase after. I tried to tell you."

"I know," said Rayna, "but surely there's something you can do to make him go away!"

"I just don't know," hedged Genene. "You could make matters worse. There is a banishing spell, but it could backfire. And there's always the Rule of Three to consider…" She recited: *Ever mind the Rule of Three, three times what thou givest returns to thee, this lesson well, thou must learn, thee only gets what thou dost earn."*

"That sounds an awful lot like 'what goes around comes around…'" said Rayna.

"Yes, and since it took the first spell so long to work, it may also take the counter spell that same time. Have you thought why this man only came to you when he was so intoxicated that he could not speak? There is symbolism here, Rayna. He was never meant for you. It would've been an unhappy coupling."

"Now I know that! I just want to get rid of him before he destroys my life anymore!"

"Well, there is another spell that could help dispel a romantic entanglement, but like I said, it's risky because it is difficult to break. It can alter a person's free will, and can bring on bad Karma for you. And you don't need anymore of that."

So eventually Rayna found herself off to the store shopping for a black candle this time. She bought the banishing oil from Genene, and the paper did not have to be of any specific source or quality. Now she just had to deal with the calls until the full moon was again upon her—and this was not easy since the moon cycles did not seem to affect the obsession that Brad had with her.

It was becoming increasingly more difficult to keep the strange encounters from her new boyfriend. She'd told him about the stalking, but had conveniently left out the part about the witch thing. Josh was an understanding sort, but how could she ever explain that she'd placed a spell on someone to make him love her. Wouldn't he then think that she'd do the same thing to him? Or maybe that she already had? Oh, the spell thing had been such a big mistake. Why hadn't she listened to Genene when she'd tried to warn her off?

Rayna had to concede that what was done was done and that she'd just have to suffer the consequences of her actions quietly and without anyone else knowing. Thus her charade began. The idea was to make sure that Josh was never at her house on Sunday night into Monday morning, for these incidents always occurred at the same time. Whatever she had to do, this was a night where she could not have him there at her apartment. In fact, she'd have to make sure that, if she was spending time with Josh, that Brad didn't follow her and then traumatize her at other locations. Hopefully, she'd make it to the full moon undiscovered, do the banishing spell, and then, with any luck, the spell would work quickly. At least *before* she went nuts.

†††††††††††††††

On the night of the full moon, Rayna set up her makeshift alter again. Only this time, she pushed the red candle and the box aside. Very carefully she wrote Brad's name on a piece of parchment stationary paper and placed it beneath the black candle. She took the Banishing Oil and softly anointed it with downward strokes. Finally, she lit the candle.

The next part was super important according to Genene. She must focus strongly on having Brad leave her alone—there must be no weakness. It had to be the strongest intent she could muster.

She began the chant.

I do not want you in my life
Your attention causes me too much strife
Leave me be without delay
This, my wish, you will obey.

I mean you no harm, just leave me alone
Your acquaintance I must now disown.

So Mote It Be

She let the candle burn for about five minutes, concentrating all the while on her intentions towards Brad; then she blew it out. Genene had advised that most times this spell worked quickly, but that she might have to repeat it once a day until the candle was all used up. She wasn't going to take chances and wait to see if it worked. She was going to do the new spell everyday just to be on the safe side.

That following Sunday night, she kept her fingers crossed and fell asleep on the couch with great trepidation. This time, she did not turn off either of her phones, though she kept the deadbolt latched on her door. Would he call? Or would the spell work?

She awoke at just before 3 a.m. with a terrible premonition. Something was going to happen, something involving her love life. *Oh no,* she thought, getting up from the couch and peeking out the window to the back parking lot of her complex. *What if he shows up again instead of using the telephone? I don't want to deal with the neighbors and the local police again...*

She went out into the kitchen to get herself a glass of milk, cursing under her breath. This man had ruined her life. Yes, yes, it was her fault she'd put that stupid spell on him, but who knew there was a Josh in the world and who knew that Brad was a crazy drunk? But of course the lesson here was one on consequences. You do the crime, you pay the fine, or do the time—or some such police motto that was fitting, if a bit infuriating at the moment.

Suddenly, she was pulled from her thoughts—the phone was ringing. Glancing up at the clock, she noted that it was (again) three in the morning exactly. Rayna grabbed the phone from its cradle and screamed into it. "Stop calling me in the middle of the night you jerk! I'm sick of it and of you!"

There was a pause on the other end as she waited for Brad to start his wailing tirade again. "Rayna?" said a male voice tentatively. "Are you all right?"

"Josh?" Rayna said into the phone, shock registering in her tone. "Josh, is that you?"

"Well, yeah…who were you expecting to call with the way you answered? Has Brad still been bothering you?"

Rayna felt a crushing weight fall down on her shoulders. Now she would have to tell Josh the whole story. She had to, because she wasn't going to lie to him. Relationships were not built on lies. It was one thing not to tell him about the infuriating Brad, but quite another to lie by just saying she was not to blame—at least in part. Guilty by omission—another police thing.

Just as she was about to spill the whole story right there on the telephone, the pounding started at her door. "Rayna!!! Let me in, please, please. I'll be good, I won't leave you!" Who else? Brad. His timing was impeccable. So much for counter-spells.

Josh was pulling her attention back to the telephone. "Who is that, Rayna?! Is it that cop again?! Let me get off the phone so I can call the police! I'm coming over there!"

Rayna hung up the phone and plopped on the couch, leaving the screaming and crying maniac in her hallway to his whimpering business. *So recap*, she thought in her mind: *Josh now knows that something is going on beyond what I've told him. Brad is outside her door crying. Josh—and the police—are on the way. The night from hell was beginning.*

††††††††††††††

After work the next afternoon, Gina and Rayna sat at Razorbacks Bar talking about the spell situation.

"Oh, it was a fiasco, alright," Rayna was saying. "Josh can't believe I did what I did and I can tell he's having second thoughts about us now. The management at the complex says that one more police incident in the middle of the night and I'm being thrown out. They hauled Brad away and he hadn't a clue why he was even at my apartment. Oh, it's all just one lovely mess."

Gina, obviously at a loss for words, just nodded and continued to sip her drink. Finally, she offered, "Well, you gonna keep doing the counter-spell till the candle burns down?"

"I guess I have to, doncha think? I mean, the damn thing worked in the first place—albeit in a sick kind of way. I have to do something..."

Gina looked up with raised eyebrows. "What about this coming Sunday? What do you think will happen? Is Josh staying over with you or is he heading for the hills."

"I think he's coming over. Though I know he's not happy about it. I'll just have to take my lumps. If I lose him over this, well, then it wasn't meant to be."

"It was Brad who wasn't meant to be...and forcing that issue screwed up your whole life," Gina surmised.

"Consequences and intentions...not good bedfellows," whispered Rayna.

Epilog

Within a couple weeks, the counter love spell did finally work and Brad stopped calling every Sunday night at three in the morning and causing havoc in Rayna's life. However, there is a hitch to the story. Brad didn't call every week; true. That was over with. But, once a year, no matter where the now-married Rayna and Josh lived, no matter how many times they changed addresses and phone numbers, no matter how hard they tried to hide, on the anniversary of the spell, the phone rang four times at three in the morning—and this has been happening for over ten years.

I've learned specifically from Wiccan friends that anyone can perform a spell, but that such caution is needed for what happened to Rayna can certainly happen to others. For example, Marla Brooks, a practicing witch living in the entertainment capital of Hollywood, asked me as she was writing her book, *Workplace Spells*, to try a spell to see if it would work. The spell? Sending Negativity Back.

She advised that it was not uncommon for people to fall victim to jealous co-workers who wanted one out of the picture or just people who were down right annoying and causing you issues throughout your workday. Her spell was designed to reflect negative energies back to the sender. The spell required that a mirror be prepared (charged) and then placed in an out of the way spot but aimed towards the person trying doing the undermining.

But it was her caution that worried me—well that and the fact that there was no particular negativity I needed to send back to anyone. "It's very important," she said, "that you not look into the mirror once it has been charged."

This is when I knew that I wouldn't be trying this spell. You do know that as soon as someone tells you not to do something, there is a devil sitting on your shoulder telling you to do that very thing. (*Look in the mirror, look in the mirror!*) So, these spells, even for good, should be carefully thought out and not used arbitrarily. It's just not worth the backlash that might occur. Take care and maybe think twice before even trying something like this. Remember Rayna.

The moral? A cliché, but true: Be careful what you wish for. You just might get it. Oh, and be careful when casting spells!

Author note: I'm not kidding here. Spells can backfire. I must say that I cannot be held responsible for any such practice! So don't blame me....

Chapter Eight

Middle River Cries

Middle River

"While ghosts may be alarming or downright scary, when you live in a haunted house, sometimes you can get used to ghostly visitors."

— Melissa Rowell and Amy Lynwander, *Baltimore's Harbor Haunts*

Amelia found all that the group was doing and everything they were lugging into her house interesting. The idea of a group hunting ghosts was not something she herself would have ever thought of—or even thought as possible until a couple weeks ago. Still, here they were in her house with equipment she'd never seen (much less understood) and showing all the professionalism of folks doing a job that had to be done... and loving it.

Amelia was well-known for her quiet manner and not much of a talker, but that didn't seem to bother the ghost hunters. They went about their business in a calm but assertive way, moving around her as though she were not even there. One young woman had stopped directly in front of her at one point, though, looking up in question at her. Amelia had quickly stepped out of the way and the woman had gone on about her business.

It was difficult not to get in their way as they worked. There were four people practically bumping into each other in her very small house that was built in the forties with tiny rooms cut up into an eclectic floor plan except for the kitchen, which was very large. Two women and two men, all dressed in shabby, easy-to-move-in clothing that made Amelia frown, scooted about taking notes and placing equipment. She wouldn't be caught dead looking like that in public, but she hated to be critical towards those there to help her.

Wires were everywhere it seemed. But it didn't seem to bother this group. She'd learned quite a bit about them and their process as she watched them from the corner of the room, well out of the way, making sure not to get under foot unless absolutely necessary—though she was so curious. She'd even began to understand most of their equipment—if not how it worked, then what it was used for at least. The group set up cameras in strategic locations to take moving pictures of any ghostly activity that passed before them—one in the hallway leading upstairs to her room, one in the parlor facing the fireplace, and another upstairs in the hallway pointed inside the baby's room.

They were very quiet putting the equipment up and that impressed her. After all, the baby was sleeping and it would not be good to wake him yet again. She'd had such a tiresome time the prior evening as he'd awakened and cried mostly all night. Colic, she'd supposed. At least that's what she wanted to believe. Amelia frowned, afraid to think what she'd been thinking might be in her house—and what her baby must be seeing. But he was sleeping calmly now. No need to worry. And this nice group of people were here to help them.

The group whispered amongst themselves as they worked and that was a blessing. It was nice to be respected. It was difficult, though, not to step forward from time to time to take a look at some of the interesting props they had. Just what was this thing with a red tip? Amelia moved closer to the woman holding it.

"EMF's hot," the woman said out loud. "Four point five. Five. Six point five. Seven." She held it out directly in front of her for Amelia to see. The red tip was flashing like a beacon and the small hand-held device was beeping. Interesting this was. She reached forward to touch the end of it. There was no jolt of electricity or any heat present—nothing to make her understand how it worked. As the woman moved it away from her, she stepped back, giving those who'd gathered around a look that said, "Sorry! Didn't mean to interrupt."

But they were not angry with her. After all, she'd asked them to come. And they were so busy with their contraptions anyway.

"Something's definitely here," said the other woman, who they called Amy. "I feel it. It's in that far corner," she said pointing to the corner behind Amelia.

Amelia turned to look and a shiver raced up her spine. She'd been right. There was something there—here that is. In her house. Something ghostly. And though she was only cognizant of it from time to time, little Timmy, her baby, was very aware. He cried every time it was around. It was up to no good, she was sure. And she wanted it gone.

One of the men stepped around her and put a tape recorder on the windowsill. "Maybe we'll catch an EVP down here. Get that ghost's voice on tape!"

Barbara, the woman who was the psychic, just nodded, as did Amelia. Amelia studied this woman. She'd never seen a self-proclaimed psychic before, until the prior week that is, though she'd heard people talk about them. One could never tell if they were fake or not, but this group seemed to trust the woman.

Barbara looked directly at her. "My name's Barbara...and you are...Amelia?"

"Yes," said Amelia. "I'm the one who asked you to come; don't you remember?" It had been a week earlier at a séance held across the street at what used to be an abandoned house. Now there were people living there, and she had gone to the séance. An interesting evening. But some of the things that were talked about were close to being sacrilegious—such personal things discussed out in the open like that! Still, it had led to this group of ghost hunters coming to her lovely home to assist her with something dark that was now residing there.

"You're gonna want to see this," called out one of the men, making Barbara turn away again from Amelia. Everyone went to the basement door.

Amelia cringed. She hated the basement. It was huge, covering the entire lower level of the house. And she was pretty sure that this was where whatever had come into the house to scare her was living. She never went down there anymore, as each time, a darkness came over her that was so threatening that she felt she would go mad. This only had to happen twice for her to know that this was not a place for her to be.

At the basement door, the man they called Eric held out one of the EMF meters and it was registering very high according to the looks on their faces. They all pulled these meters out from the equipment that they carried hooked to varied parts of their bodies and in pockets that seemed to just appear on their clothing. They were shooting photographs with cameras all over the area as well and she had to flinch when the man, John, shot a flash nearly right into her eyes.

Amelia leaned forward to look over the shoulders of the people at the door way, just as Barbara said, "Amelia doesn't like it down there."

Wow, thought Amelia, *she really is psychic.* She'd not said a word to them about the basement.

But as the group started down the dark basement stairs, she hung back. She was not going down there. She just couldn't.

Barbara looked over her shoulder at her, "It's okay, you just wait here. We'll be all right."

Amelia merely nodded, but had her doubts.

††††††††††††††

That prior week at the séance, Barbara had at first been skeptical. The group was made up of about six women plus her paranormal research group that consisted of herself, Amy, John, and Eric. The hostess had called her, quite excited to employ her to do readings for her and her friends. It wasn't really a séance, but the women wanted to call it that. It was merely an evening of entertainment with incoming funds that would help offset the cost of conducting serious paranormal investigations for her group. A necessary evil that was often fun.

Barbara had noticed the frail young woman immediately and felt her discomfort being around all the women who were so casually laughing and enjoying the evening. She remained quiet, though, and went about setting the stage for the readings. She placed a tape recorder in the middle of the coffee table that sat in the center of the small living room. Opening a new package of cassette tapes, she set them next to the recorder. Each person she read for would be afforded a copy of her reading to take home and listen to at a later time.

The evening progressed with Barbara reading the first three women, spending about a half hour with each. She went into relationships and even into the depths of sexual developments for one of the women. She talked of career moves and backstabbing work plots to suppress the women there. She predicted children and talked about school issues for parents in the group. It was a mixed bag and the women were having a grand-old time.

After reading for the first three women, Barbara suggested a break so that she could go to the bathroom, have something to drink, and to generally relax before moving forward. The women were all ready to take a few minutes and proceeded to the large kitchen to snack on the foods they'd prepared just for this occasion—as well as to take a nip or two of some of the blackberry wine made available to them.

Barbara didn't join the ladies in the kitchen, however; rather, once she'd taken care of nature's business, she sat in the recliner with her head tilted back and eyes closed. It was then that the shy Amelia approached her.

"Forgive me for interrupting your break…" she began and then trailed off. "I didn't like talking in front of the others."

Barbara smiled. "Hello there, you're not interrupting me. And I certainly understand you're not wanting to chat in front of them. Very risqué at times, wasn't it? I'm thinking that you need my help." She opened her eyes. "What can I do for you?"

"Would it be too much trouble to ask you to come to my home? I'm afraid that there's…*something*…going on there. My home might be haunted. And it's beginning to frighten me."

So it was then that Barbara made the arrangements to visit Amelia the following week with her team.

"Thank you ever so much," said Amelia. Then she looked toward the window and careened her neck to look out. "I believe I hear my baby. He's crying. I should go."

"You have a baby? You should've brought him," said Barbara.

"Well, he was sleeping and the nanny was with him. But I should go now. Thank you again!"

Just then, Barbara's attention was drawn back to a woman who entered from the kitchen. "Barbara, you really should come out and sample some of the goodies! It can only help your readings!"

Barbara laughed and stood, noticing the front door ajar and Amelia gone. She closed the door and retired to the kitchen.

†††††††††††††††

Amelia peered down the dingy stairwell to the basement, but was unable to force herself to follow the ghost group down the plank steps into the darkness. Well, it wasn't exactly dark, but dim to be sure, and a definite feeling of dread welled up in her throat telling her it wasn't a good idea no matter the kind of light.

She could hear them very clearly though, and it didn't sound good.

"There's something here alright. Amelia was right. And it's not a good spirit either. There's violence hooked to this one and it's out for blood," she heard Barbara say. "It won't talk with me though. I can't get a handle on what it wants or why it's here. But I will..."

The man called John said, "Do you hear a baby crying?"

Amelia instantly moved back from the doorway and listened for Timmy—maybe he'd woken and his cries could be heard through the pipes. But she didn't hear him. She went back to the doorway and stepped down one step to the basement. Her curiosity was greater than her fear at this moment, and she felt safe with these ghost hunters in her midst. She took another step down, and another.

Soon, while not completely in the basement, she could see the group and what they were doing. This was far enough.

"Look," said Eric, pointing to the corner of the room, "there!"

Amelia peered into the corner and she saw *it* just as the others saw it. A black mist was floating, shape shifting into varied cloudy forms. Her heart jumped to her throat. It was him. It was that man. It was that ... murderer? She frowned. Where had that word come from? How did she know this shape, this cloud of whirling vapor?

The group scattered about her basement was moving fast now, taking photographs, using their flashing equipment that beeped, and taking moving pictures. It was important, they said, that they document everything. She didn't know why. It was only important to her that they get rid of the thing. It traumatized her and little Timmy. But her heart was beating too hard to think about it and she ran upstairs knowing that her child would be crying now.

††††††††††††††

Once upstairs, Amy said, "What's that sound? And where's Amelia now?"

They all stopped to listen to the creaking sounds coming from above them, a very rhythmic sound, almost comforting—a rocking chair, its wooden runners squeaking back and forth on the old wood.

"I hear a baby crying, too. And it sounds like the same cry I heard at the séance party last week on that one woman's tape when she played it back. Remember?" asked Barbara.

Eric had gone to the stairs and bounded up a story. He called down in a raspy whisper, "It's not on this level. It's coming from the attic."

The entire ghost group made its way up the narrow stairway to the second floor and stood beneath the location where the chair was rocking in the attic above. Although all of them could hear the squeaking sound of the rocker and were holding their recorders high toward the ceiling to capture the sounds, only Barbara could hear the soft whimpering of a child and the tiny voice of the woman singing a lullaby.

"Amelia is up there," she said quietly, "and she's singing to little Timmy to calm him."

It was then that they heard a loud crash coming from the recesses of the house—in the basement. They all looked at each other with startled expressions.

"Now what was that?" Eric said moving back to the stairwell and peering down.

"That's the ghost of whoever murdered Amelia and the baby," answered Barbara.

†††††††††††††††

It was late in the evening that Barbara sat on the floor of the dusty attic, noting that no one had been in the dark and dank place for some time. The rest of the group was downstairs monitoring her with video cameras as she prepared to talk to Amelia. Barbara sat quietly, eyes closed, and breath deep.

"Amelia?" she said. "Come talk with me. You don't have to be afraid. Remember, you asked us to come...to help you."

The quiet room now filled with the creaking of a rocking chair. Downstairs, Barbara could hear the others who were excited that they, too, could hear the rocker and could also see a shadow—blurry as it was—on the monitoring screen.

Barbara knew though that Amelia was present. "Hello Amelia; we're sorry for all the mess to your home. But you know that we're here to help, don't you?" She could see the woman in her mind's eye using the psychic gifts that were so strong in her. Amelia was a small woman, and young—not more than about twenty-two. And she held her baby close to her breast as she rocked in the chair.

"I know you are here to help," Amelia replied, "but all of you are so strange..."

"We're from another time, Amelia," said Barbara. "And we've come to help you cross over."

There was a frown of confusion on Amelia's face as she looked out and around the room. "I don't understand."

Barbara nodded. "I know you don't, so let me help you to understand. First, I need to talk with you about what's in the basement."

Barbara could see Amelia go stiff and a terror showed on her face that made Barbara flinch. This was not going to be easy. But then it never was in these kind of cases. "Amelia," she began again, "the shadow person we saw in the basement...that is the ghost of a man who killed you and little Timmy some time in the forties, we think. Right around the time that this house was first built. His ghost is stuck there because not only was he evil, but you will not let him go."

"Me!" cried Amelia. "I don't want him here!" Then the rocker stopped as the full impact of Barbara's statement hit her. "You said that I was killed by this man. And Timmy, too." She looked down at her own body, fully formed in her eyes, but only a smoky film to Barbara. "I'm not dead. Surely you can see that..."

"Amelia," Barbara began again. "Yes, you have passed on, too. And your spirit is held here because you don't know you're dead and you are still living in fear of the man who killed you in the basement of this house."

Amelia seemed to float above Barbara now, a mist that she could physically see in addition to the form she saw in her third eye. "Yes," relented Amelia. "Now I understand. And I remember. I was here, alone with Timmy. Timmy was here in his room—I'd made the attic a lovely nursery. There's plenty of room here, as you can see. That man broke in, but I didn't know it and I went down into the basement to get some pickled relish I'd jarred…and he was there…and he … strangled me… And I could hear little Timmy crying upstairs..."

Barbara could hear Amelia sobbing and wondered if the sound would record on their recorders. "Amelia?" she said. "You don't have to stay here any longer. You and Timmy can cross over now; we've banished the spirit in the basement. There's no longer a need for you to be here. Do you see the light?"

"Leave here? Leave my home?" Amelia was shaking her head in a negative way.

The mist was swirling. "Yes," said Barbara. "The new owners of the house will take care of it for you. They've been hearing you rocking Timmy every night ever since they moved in. They hear your sobbing and Timmy's crying. And they've had a fear of the basement, too. But the basement is clear now, and you and Timmy are safe. It's time to move on to the next world—the next life. A better one awaits you and Timmy."

"Really? Do you think so? For me and Timmy?"

"Yes, it's time to go, Amelia."

Barbara watched as the mist swirled a bit more and in her third eye she saw Amelia stand with Timmy in her arms.

"I believe you and I trust you," Amelia said to Barbara. "Thank you for helping me."

With that, the mist dissipated and Amelia and her baby disappeared from Barbara's vision. They had crossed over.

Epilog

The house on Middle River Road was torn down some years later and the person telling me about the rocking chair ghost and the crying child believes that townhouses now occupy the property. One can only wonder if the ghost continues to visit folks in the new homes, rocking late into the night and singing to a crying child.

The actual séance took place across the alley, though the rocking chair incidents were heard every night at the original house. The neighbor's home did indeed produce a tape with the cry of a newborn baby faintly heard in the background of the psychic talking. There were no children present for the evening and no one heard the sound during the séance. It was only when the women were playing the cassette tapes for their husbands later that night that the crying baby surfaced. Also, oddly, as soon as one of the tapes began to play, the sound of a heartbeat could be heard—*thump, thump…thump, thump*. When the voices of those in the room began, the sounds went away.

Later that same evening, after everyone went home, the owner of the house across the alley heard the slamming of a door—the outside door. When checked, nothing was disturbed and it was thought that the rocking ghost and her baby had visited the neighbor's house that evening possibly to ask for help from the psychic.

A Haunting Conclusion

"In some cases, spirits are defined as the part of us that separates from our bodies after we die and move on to the next world, perhaps after a quick stop to let loved ones know that we're okay, or to give a message. Ghosts, on the other hand, stick around."

— Marcy Italiano, *Spirits and Death in Niagara*

Questions:

† *What about the people who actually see, feel, or experience paranormal manifestations in one form or another?*

† *Is there correlation or connection between the other world and these particular individuals?*

As I've researched the material for this and other paranormal books and conducted interviews with those who have seen things from the world beyond, I've found that in most cases, their sightings are not merely hooked to the places I've investigated. Their experiences seem to infiltrate their daily lives—wherever they go.

It's as though they've opened a door in their minds that allow them to perceive things just outside the "normal" bustling world. If someone sees or hears a ghost at one of the locations you've read about in this book—or anyplace for that matter—in most cases that person with the story will have also had other experiences at other locations. Several people have told me that ghosts hitch rides with their intended "hauntee" and, therefore, can be sensed in varied unorthodox places. I'm all too aware of another ghost investigator who brought the ghost of a bank robber home with her. It didn't bother her specifically, but caused havoc with her animals, to the point of a full family meltdown.

In other words, ghosts can be hooked to a place as we've all been taught to believe; but it also appears that ghosts can attach to a person and travel right along as a companion on the other side. Sometimes good; sometimes bad.

Still another thought stems from the actual opening up of intuitive powers that allows a person to see or feel something ghostly after an initial occurrence. I can only surmise by the research that both these theories are correct. I have personal evidence of that as I have become "aware" of many more premonitions, "knowings," "coincidences" (really synchronicity because I don't believe in coincidence any longer), and plain good ole ghostly activities. This is just because I'm more open to the possibilities of a world and life beyond this one. If you open up your senses, you will be rewarded with … something.

One thing that I found constant while researching and recounting these stories was that people asked the same questions of me. I took some time to talk with psychic Laurie Hull, founder of Delaware County Paranormal Research (Pennsylvania), about some of these topics.

† *Why do you think ghosts still hang around places?*

Well, some of them can't accept that they are dead—some are very attached to material things and can't let go. Some stay around because they have something they wanted to do and it didn't get done. There's like a million reasons—as many reasons as people do anything. Some spirits stay because they want to get back at somebody. Some stay because they are afraid of seeing somebody on the other side. Some are afraid of going to hell on the other side. You just have to talk to them. I say talk, but it's more in your mind, it goes back and forth. And I've gotten in the habit of saying everything out loud because we want to get everything on tape, but people can't hear the ghost so I have to say what the ghosts say too.

...We don't understand everything in the world. They were here before we were here. It would be like someone coming in my house and saying, 'Leave.' I'd say, 'Yeah right.' It's like a person without a body. You can talk to it like a person. It has feelings like a person. They can be crazy like a person. They can be angry, sad, happy...crazy is scary.

Some ghosts are still in the moment of their deaths, which is upsetting for anyone who is sensitive to it. Which is why people sometimes get really scared or upset, and some people start crying because you get (emotions) projected on you and they connect with you on that emotion and it completely fills your body. And then you are terrified and scared and you feel you just have to get out of there.

Another reason for them to stay that I didn't mention: If someone dies and you really love that person and you can't stop thinking about them and you miss them so much—and wish they were back, they can't leave. You won't let go of them. And sometimes they stay because you are so devastated that they feel bad and they will be stuck. So I try to tell people to let go of this person because they don't belong here and they need to move on. And nobody can move on as long as the spirit is still there. You're still stuck because you think of them all the time, because they are there. And they are stuck here.

> They can also come back to say hello once in a while. There are whole books written about just that. Sometimes they will come back to help you if something is wrong. Sometimes they come back if something is going on that they don't like. A lot of people communicate with them in a dream.

For me, I've been involved with all of the above. But the paranormal (or is it really normal and we don't know it yet?) doesn't seem to stop there. Spirit guides, animal communications, telepathy (or ESP), deep meditation, demonology, and witchcraft all come into play when it comes to questions of the otherworld.

And I hope that this book of ghostly stories sparks your interest into some of these topics and that you yourself will delve into the world of hauntings in Baltimore County and beyond!

Appendix

The following information is provided by author and ghost investigator, Fiona Broome and appears in her book, *Ghosts of Austin, Texas.* For more information, visit http://hollowhill.com.

Fiona's Top Places to Find Ghosts

No matter where you are, certain locations are usually haunted. These sites don't always have ghosts, but they're the best places to start when you're looking for unreported visitors from beyond the grave.

Theatres

Ghosts tend to frequent places where people have performed on stage. These include movie theatres that were once performance halls.

There are three kinds of ghosts at these locations:

† The actor who is still seen on or near the stage...

† The stagehand that lingers backstage, usually around the lighting or the curtain controls...

† Finally, someone who appears towards the back of the hall, especially during rehearsals. He or she almost always smokes a cigarette that people can smell, or they'll see the smoke or the burning ember.

Battlegrounds

Almost every battleground has some residual energy from the violent and tragic deaths that occurred there. Some battlegrounds are actually haunted by the spirits of the men and women who died there, too. Between Texas' battles for independence, Indian attacks, and Civil War conflicts, you'll find many locations with ghost stories… and *real* ghosts.

Cemeteries

It's a cliché but a true one: Ghosts haunt cemeteries. Modern graves—burials that occurred less than fifty years ago—are rarely haunted for very long.

For the most powerful hauntings, look for graves that are at least a hundred years old. Only a few are haunted, but you'll find elevated EMF levels at many of the graves, especially if they're unmarked.

Colleges

Almost every college or university reports at least one ghost. Most also report poltergeist phenomena. The performing arts center is often the most haunted location on campus.

Summer Camps

Most camps—especially Scout camps—have a ghost or two. Usually, these are benevolent ghosts of former camp counselors or the camp manager. An aroma of perfume or pipe smoke is usually reported, related to someone who worked there.

Very Old, Large Homes and Buildings

Like most ancient castles, many very old, large buildings have ghosts. In an older home, a woman who lived there lingers to be sure that the house and its occupants remain safe. She usually wears a green dress.

Another ghost is mad and lurks in the attic, basement, or an outbuilding. A variation on this is a ghost in the nearby woods or a field next to an old homestead. These hauntings are almost predictable.

Old Hotels

Many hotels are haunted by the same people who visited them in life. They're usually happy ghosts who return to relax and enjoy themselves.

Classic haunted spots in hotels include the top floor, the elevator, and the lobby. This is true of the Driskill Hotel in Austin, Texas; its most haunted and elegant hotel, and a favorite destination for visiting ghost hunters.

This category of haunting extends to former brothels. In the late nineteenth century, dozens of feisty, independent-minded madams owned "boarding houses." Today, these sites are often clubs, bars, and restaurants in the entertainment and warehouse districts—and most of them have great ghost stories to share.

Hospitals, Retirement Homes, Morgues and Funeral Parlors

As you'd expect, some people aren't willing to leave the last place where they were seen and called by name. However, if these sites are still in use, they're usually off-limits to ghost hunters.

Instead, look for former locations of these kinds of buildings. They're usually haunted by perplexed and sometimes angry ghosts.

Fiona's Tips for Taking Great Ghost Photos

† **Avoid lens flares.** Don't point the lens towards the sun, light, a full moon, or any reflective surface. At least 80% of the orb photos that I review are clearly reflections from shiny surfaces or lights that are in the frame of the photo or just outside it.

† **Don't take pictures in high humidity or rain**. Moisture in the air can result in dozens—even hundreds—of orbs in a single photo. If you see too many orbs in your pictures, or many very tiny orbs among larger ones, they're probably from rain or high humidity.

† **Watch out for bugs.** Your ghost-hunting companion should watch for insects in front of the camera as you take pictures.

Genuine orbs are almost perfectly round. If the orb is oval, irregularly shaped, or has blurry borders, it's probably an insect.

† **Avoid smoke.** Tests show that smoke causes fewer eerie effects than most researchers guessed, smoke. However, even if you can't see or smell it when you're taking your photos it can cause misty figures.

† **Keep your camera strap and hair out of the way.**

† **Always take two photos in a row**, moving as little as possible between the clicks of the camera's shutter. If your picture shows an actual anomaly, it will usually appear in only one photo. If it looks almost exactly the same (size, brightness, location) in both pictures, it's probably a reflection or a hovering insect.

† **Save all of your pictures** until you've seen at least a dozen with orbs and anomalies. Until you know what you're looking for, you may not realize how many anomalies are in your photos.

If you use a film camera, the photo lab may adjust the contrast to prevent the orbs (and other anomalies) from "spoiling" your photos. Sometimes, you have to study the negatives to find the orbs.

I've taken hundreds of photos that clearly show orbs on the negative, but those same orbs are easily overlooked on the print. It took years of practice to spot these orbs without referring to the negatives.

When you realize how faint some orbs are, you'll probably find dozens of overlooked "ghosts" in your pictures.

†††††††††††††††

Ghost Ropes

As I researched the ghost stories of Baltimore County, it was interesting to note that most people I talked to ask questions that involve the identification and investigation process for ghost hunting. They want to know:

† How can I tell if there is really a ghost here?
† How will I know if it's a true paranormal phenomena or something natural?
† Can you tell me what's haunting my property?
† Can I hunt my own ghost? How do I do that?
† What are all those things [equipment] the guys on television use to hunt ghosts? How do they work? Do you use them?

My answer, at one time was, "I'm not a ghost investigator, but I'll see what I can do to find out what you'd like to know." But before I knew it, I was intricately involved with a real-live ghost group—the Chester County Paranormal Research Society (CCPRS), a non-profit organization based out of West Chester, Pennsylvania, where I currently reside (though Baltimore County has been my home for at least thirty years of my life). Coupled with scientific methods and experience, this is a group of investigators researching in an attempt to validate and prove the existence of paranormal activity. It was this group who taught me the ghostly ropes of paranormal investigations. (And to be honest, though I'm happy to be along to help prove the existence of the paranormal, I really just want to experience it—since I personally already know it exists. I don't care a lot about what other people believe. It is what it is.)

Since, most people had questions about the stories and ghosts that haunted them, I decided that this would be a good place to explain the process of a true investigation and relate some of the terminology and equipment used. Though you may not have seen some of these terms in the stories as told here, when scientific functions are applied to the tales for investigation, these terms and equipment items are used.

†††††††††††††††

The following was written by and offered courtesy of Scott Lefebvre, author of *Spooky Creepy Long Island*.

Guide for Urban Exploration

If you're anything like me, creepy looking abandoned buildings have an almost irresistible attraction as destinations for adventurous excursions.

Attractive destinations include abandoned buildings, usually the older the better, and especially asylums and churches, ex-military bases, and anything else interesting and off limits.

Many urban explorers bring back small souvenirs from their excursions. I still have two coffee mugs from the Ladd Center, which are precious to me. But I ask that if you do decide to visit someplace with the purpose of exploring it, that you avoid the urge to destroy or vandalize anything while you're there. Please think about preserving the site for other explorers. Vandalism only serves to increase security surveillance or make the site more likely to face destruction as a safety hazard and a popular destination for unwanted visitors. It's perfectly acceptable to take as many pictures as you desire, but the best souvenir will be your memory of the experience.

Things That You Might Want to Do or Remember to Bring Along With You

Light

If your planned destination is a building, whether day or night, you'll want to bring a **flashlight**. If you enter an abandoned building, there will most likely be rooms that do not have direct access to the outside and will be dark without artificial light. It's also important to always be able to see where you're planning on going. The most common injuries for urban explorers are tripping over something underfoot because they weren't watching where they were going, or hitting their head or getting cut by something hanging down from overhead.

My favorite flashlight is the Mag-Lite mini. It's more expensive than the one-use flashlights that you can buy at the register or get for free as a promotional item with a pack of batteries, but it's infinitely more reliable and durable. It will survive a few accidental drops onto concrete floors, and the bulbs are cheap and replaceable. The light it throws is bright and clear and adjustable, and it's relatively cheap, so it won't be a big deal if you drop it someplace that you can't easily retrieve it. It runs on double A batteries and gets pretty good battery life, but **make sure you bring spare batteries**. You don't want to be trapped in an unfamiliar, potentially dangerous environment with a dead flashlight.

Photography

A **camera** with a good flash is also highly recommended. Digital cameras are lighter and often cheaper than film cameras and can take a lot of pictures without requiring the user to play around with loading in a new roll of film in a dusty, musty environment. Plus, if you have to run, you don't want a bulky film camera with a flash attachment bumping around. Some of the most common sad stories about urban exploration are about broken or lost film cameras. Don't be one of those people.

Hair

Tying back long hair and wearing a baseball hat is recommended. You don't want your hair to accidentally get snagged on something and get pulled out. If you're going to hit your head on something it's better to get your hat knocked off than to get a rusty cut. Additionally, a stray hair flashed in front of a camera lens is frequently mistaken for evidence of the presence of the supernatural—a common and embarrassing error, and easily avoidable with a little precaution.

Attire

Wear **sensible shoes**—sneakers with thick, skid-proof soles, or even better, work boots. The floors of abandoned buildings are often cluttered with debris and filth and sometimes damp or flooded. Also keep in mind that you may have to avoid wild animals or other hazards, so please be smart and tie your shoes. But only run if you're outside. Even a familiar spot might have changed since the last time you were there. Running in an unfamiliar environment is easily the best way to accidentally and possibly seriously hurt yourself while urban exploring.

You may want to bring light **work gloves**. Not so much to avoid leaving fingerprints, but more because abandoned buildings can be dirty places. There are rusty ladders and stairwell handrails and the walls are usually moldy. Anywhere you put your hands you can pick up dirt and you don't want that kind of dirt in your eyes or mouth. It's better to get your glove snagged on something sharp instead of cutting your hand open.

Just for Your Health

And speaking of mold and dust, if you're predisposed to allergies, you may want to invest in a good **dust mask**. In some old buildings there's lead paint dust and asbestos. I'm not too worried about breathing in a little toxic dust, but some of you may not be so careless.

The Legalities

Finally, we all know that **trespassing is illegal**. If you're uncomfortable with possible legal involvement, there are many excellent places of supernatural interest that are perfectly legal to visit and explore.

It's important to keep in mind that even going onto a property that is not public can be considered trespassing. Entering an abandoned building can be considered illegal entry and trespassing. And if you had to do anything to a window or door to get into a building, it becomes breaking and entering.

On a final note, I implore you to NOT bring any **weapons** along with you while urban exploring. Having a small pocketknife or pocket multi-tool like a Swiss Army Knife or a Leatherman can be convenient and handy, especially if your hair or clothes get snagged and you have to cut yourself loose. But it's completely unnecessary to bring a big hunting knife, or even worse, a handgun, along for the trip. If you're looking for ghosts, a weapon won't do you any good against them. Having a weapon just makes it that much more likely that someone will accidentally get hurt, and being discovered while urban exploring just gets more complicated if you're running around with a samurai sword.

Please be smart, be safe, and send me a set of your awesome pictures.

Or even better, take me a long on your next trip.

††††††††††††††††

** The following section is provided by the Chester County Paranormal Research Society in Pennsylvania and appears in training materials for new investigators. Please visit www.ChesterCountyprs.com* for *more information.*

Glossary

Air Probe Thermometer

A thermometer with an external probe that is capable of taking instant measurements of the air temperature.

Anomalous field

A field that cannot be explained or ruled out by various possibilities, and that can be a representation of spirit or paranormal energy present.

Apparition

A transparent form of a human or animal; a spirit.

Artificial field

A field that is caused by electrical outlets, such as appliances.

Aural Enhancer

A listening device that enhances or amplifies audio signals. i.e., Orbitor Bionic Ear.

Automatic writing

The act of a spirit guiding a human agent in writing a message that is brought through by the spirit.

Base readings

The readings taken at the start of an investigation and are used as a means of comparing other readings taken later during the course of the investigation.

Demonic Haunting

A haunting that is caused by an inhuman or subhuman energy or spirit.

Dowsing Rods

A pair of L-shaped rods or a single Y-shaped rod, used to detect the presence of what the person using them is trying to find.

Electro-static generator

A device that electrically charges the air often used in paranormal investigations/research as a means to contribute to the materialization of paranormal or spiritual energy.

ELF

Extremely Low Frequency.

ELF Meter/EMF Meter
A device that measures electric and magnetic fields.

EMF
Electro Magnetic Field.

EVP
Electronic Voice Phenomena.

False positive
Something that is being interpreted as paranormal within a picture or video and is, in fact, a natural occurrence or defect of the equipment used.

Gamera
A 35mm film camera connected with a motion detector that is housed in a weatherproof container and takes a picture when movement is detected. Made by Silver Creek Industries.

Geiger Counter
A device that measures gamma and x-ray radiation.

Infra Red
An invisible band of radiation at the lower end of the visible light spectrum. With wavelengths from 750 nm to 1 mm, infrared starts at the end of the microwave spectrum and ends at the beginning of visible light. Infrared transmission typically requires an unobstructed line of sight between transmitter and receiver. Widely used in most audio and video remote controls, infrared transmission is also used for wireless connections between computer devices and a variety of detectors.

Intelligent haunting

A haunting of a spirit or other entity that has the ability to interact with the living and do things that can make its presence known.

Milli-gauss

Unit of measurement, measures in 1000th of a gauss and is named for the famous German mathematician, Karl Gauss.

Orbs

Anomalous spherical shapes that appear on video and still photography.

Pendulum

A pointed item that is hung on the end of a string or chain and is used as a means of contacting spirits. An individual will hold the item and let it hang from the fingertips. The individual will ask questions aloud and the pendulum answers by moving.

Poltergeist haunting

A haunting that has two sides, but same kinds of activity in common. Violent outbursts of activity with doors and windows slamming shut, items being thrown across a room and things being knocked off of surfaces. Poltergeist hauntings are usually focused around a specific individual who resides or works at the location of the activity reported, and, in some cases, when the person is not present at the location, activity does not occur. A poltergeist haunting may be the cause of a human agent or spirit/energy that may be present at the location.

Portal

An opening in the realm of the paranormal that is a gateway between one dimension and the next. A passageway for spirits to come and go through. See also Vortex.

Residual haunting

A haunting that is an imprint of an event or person that plays itself out like a loop until the energy that causes it has burned itself out.

Scrying

The act of eliciting information with the use of a pendulum from spirits.

Table Tipping

A form of spirit communication, the act of a table being used as a form of contact. Individuals will sit around a table and lightly place their fingertips on the edge of the table and elicit contact with a spirit. The Spirit will respond by "tipping" or moving the table.

Talking Boards

A board used as a means of communicating with a spirit. Also known as a Quija Board.

Vortex

A place or situation regarded as drawing into its center all that surrounds it.

White Noise

A random noise signal that has the same sound energy level at all frequencies.

Equipment Explanations

In this section, the CCPRS looks at the application and benefits of equipment used on investigations with greater detail. The equipment used for an investigation plays a vital role in the ability to collect objective evidence and helps to determine what is and is not paranormal activity. But a key point to be made here is: the investigator is the most important tool on any investigation. With that said, let's now take a look at the main pieces of equipment used during an investigation...

The Geiger Counter

The Geiger counter is device that measures radiation. A "Geiger counter" usually contains a metal tube with a thin metal wire along its middle. The space in between them is sealed off and filled with a suitable gas and with the wire at about +1000 volts relative to the tube.

An ion or electron penetrating the tube (or an electron knocked out of the wall by X-rays or gamma rays) tears electrons off atoms in the gas. Because of the high positive voltage of the central wire, those electrons are then attracted to it. They gain energy that collide with atoms and release more electrons, until the process snowballs into an "avalanche", producing an easily detectable pulse of current. With a suitable filling gas, the flow of electricity stops by itself, or else the electrical circuitry can help stop it.

The instrument was called a "counter" because every particle passing it produced an identical pulse, allowing particles to be counted, usually electronically. But it did not tell anything about their identity or energy, except that they must have sufficient energy to penetrate the walls of the counter.

The Geiger counter is used in paranormal research to measure the background radiation at a location. The working theory in this field is that paranormal activity can effect the background radiation. In some cases, it will increase the radiation levels and in other cases it will decrease the levels.

Digital and 35mm Film Cameras

The camera is an imperative piece of equipment that enabled us to gather objective evidence during a case. Some of the best evidence presented from cases of paranormal activity over the years has been because of photographs taken. If you own your own digital camera or 35mm film camera, you need to be fully aware of what the cameras abilities and limitations are. Digital cameras have been at the center of great debate in the field of paranormal research over the years.

The earlier incarnations of digital cameras were full of inherent problems and notorious for creating "false positive" pictures. A "false positive" picture is a picture that has anomalous elements within the picture that are the result of a camera defect or other natural occurrence. There are many pictures scattered about the Internet that claim to be of true paranormal activity, but in fact they are "false positives." Orbs, defined as anomalous paranormal energy that can show up as balls of light or streaks in still photography or video, are the most controversial pictures of paranormal energy in the field. There are so many theories (good and bad) about the origin of orbs and what they are. The pictures in the CCPRS collection that has an orb—or orbs—are not presented in a way that state that they are absolutely of paranormal nature. I have yet to capture an orb photo that made me feel certain that in fact it is of a paranormal nature.

If you use your own camera, understand that your camera is vital. I encourage all members who own their own cameras to do research on the make and model of the camera and see what other consumers are saying about them. Does the manufacturer give any info regarding possible defects or design flaws with that particular model? Understanding your camera will help to rule out the possibility of interpreting a "false positive" for an authentic picture of paranormal activity.

Video Cameras

The video camera is also a fundamental tool in the investigation as another way for collecting objective evidence that can support the proof of paranormal activity. The video camera can be used in various ways during the investigation. It can be set on a tripod and left in a location where paranormal activity has been reported. It can also be used as a hand-held camera and the investigator will take it with them during their walk through investigation as a means of documenting to hopefully capture anomalous activity on tape. Infra-Red technology has become a feature on most consumer level video cameras and depending on the manufacturer can be called "night shot" or "night alive." What this technology does is allow us to use the camera in zero light. Most cameras with this feature will add a green tint or haze to the camera when it is being used in this mode. A video camera with this ability holds great appeal to the paranormal investigator.

EMF/ELF Meters

EMF=Electro Magnetic Frequency ELF=Extremely Low Frequency

The EMF/ELF meter is a meter that measures Electric and Magnetic fields in an AC or DC current field. It measures in a unit of measurement called "milli-gauss," named for the famous German mathematician, Karl Gauss. Most meters will measure in a range of 1-5 or 1-10 milli-gauss. The reason that EMF meters are used in paranormal research is because of the theory that a spirit or paranormal energy can add to the energy field when it is materializing or is present in a location. The theory says that, typically, an energy that measures between 3-7 milli-gauss may be of a paranormal origin. This doesn't mean that an artificial field can't also measure within this range. That is why we take base readings and make maps notating where artificial fields occur. The artificial fields are a direct result of electricity, i.e. wiring, appliances, light switches, electrical outlets, circuit breakers, high voltage power lines, sub-stations, etc.

The Earth emits a naturally occurring magnetic field all around us and has an effect on paranormal activity. Geo-magnetic storm activity can also have a great influence on paranormal activity. For more information on this kind of phenomena visit: www.noaa.sec.com.

There are many different types of EMF meters; and each one, although it measures with the same unit of measurement, may react differently. An EMF meter can range from anywhere to $12 to $1,000 or more depending on the quality and features that it has. Most meters are measuring the AC (alternating current, the type of fields created by man-made electricity) fields and some can measure DC (direct current-naturally occurring fields, batteries also fall into the category of DC) fields. The benefit of having a meter that can measure DC fields is that they will automatically filter out the artificial fields created by AC fields and can pick up more naturally occurring electro magnetic fields. Some of the higher-tech EMF meters are so sensitive that they can pick up the fields generated by living beings. The EMF meter was originally designed to measure the earth's magnetic fields and also to measure the fields created by electrical an artificial means.

There have been various studies over the years about the long term effects of individuals living in or near high fields. There has been much controversy as to whether or not long-term exposure to high fields can lead to cancer. It has been proven though that no matter what, long term exposure to high fields can be harmful to your health. The ability to locate these high fields within a private residence or business is vital to the investigation. We may offer suggestions to the client as to possible solutions for dealing with high fields. The wiring in a home or business can greatly affect the possibility of high fields. If the wiring is old and/or not shielded correctly, it can emit high fields that may affect the ability to correctly notate any anomalous fields that may be present.

Audio Recording Equipment

Audio recording equipment is used for conducting EVP (Electronic Voice Phenomena) research and experiments. What is an EVP? An EVP is a phenomenon where paranormal voices or sounds can be captured with audio recording devices. The theory is that the activity will imprint directly onto the device or tape, but has not been proven to be an absolute fact. The use of an external microphone is essential when conducting EVP experiments with analog recording equipment. The internal microphone on an analog tape recorder can pick up the background noise of the working parts within the tape recorder and can taint the evidence as a whole. Most digital recorders are quiet enough to use the internal microphone, but as a general rule of thumb, we do not use them. An external microphone will be used always. Another theory about EVP research is that an authentic EVP will happen within the range 250-400hz. This is a lower frequency range and isn't easily heard by the human ear, and the human voice does not emit in this range. EVP is rarely heard at the moment it happens—it is usually revealed during the playback and analysis portion of the investigation.

Thermometers

The use of a thermometer in an investigation goes without saying. This is how we monitor the temperature changes during the course of an investigation. CCPRS is currently using Digital thermometers with remote sensors as a way to set up a perimeter and to notate any changes in a stationary location of an investigation. The Air-probe thermometer can take "real time" readings that are instantly accurate. This is the more appropriate thermometer for measuring air temperature and "cold spots" that may be caused by the presence of paranormal phenomena. The IR Non-contact thermometer is the most misused thermometer in the field of paranormal research. CCPRS does not own or use IR Non-contact thermometers for this reason. The IR (infra-red) Non-contact thermometer is meant for measuring surface temperatures from a remote location. It shoots an infrared beam out to an object and bounces to the unit and gives the temperature reading. I have seen, first hand, investigators using this thermometer as a way to measure air temperature. NO, this is not correct! Enough said. In an email conversation that I have had with Grant Wilson from TAPS, he has said that, "Any change in temperature that can't be measured with your hand is not worth notating..."

Bibliography

Balzano, Christopher. *The Bridgewater Triangle*. Atglen, Pennsylvania: Schiffer Publishing, 2008.

Boyd, Katie. Beckah Tolly. Raven Duclos. *Ghost Quest in New Hampshire*. Atglen, Pennsylvania: Schiffer Publishing, 2008

Boyd, Katie. *Devils and Demonology in the 21st Century*. Atglen, Pennsylvania: Schiffer Publishing, 2009.

Brooks, Marla. *Workplace Spells*. Atglen, Pennsylvania: Schiffer Publishing, 2009.

Gray-Cobb, Geof. *Twist Your Fate*. Atglen, Pennsylvania: Schiffer Publishing, 2008.

Holzer, Hans. *The Spirit Connection*. Atglen, Pennsylvania: Schiffer Publishing, 2008.

Italiano, Marcy, *Spirits and Death in Niagara*. Atglen, Pennsylvania: Schiffer Publishing, 2007.

Roseberry, D. P. *Cape May Haunts*. Atglen, Pennsylvania: Schiffer Publishing, 2007.

Roseberry, D. P. *Ghosts of Valley Forge and Phoenixville*. Atglen. Pennsylvania: Schiffer Publishing, 2006.

Rowell, Melissa. Amy Lunwander. *Baltimore's Harbor Haunts*. Atglen, Pennsylvania: Schiffer Publishing, 2005

Wikipedia. "Sleep Paralysis." Accessed September 19, 2008.